ISLAND GRINDS

Good Food, Real Value,
and Local Atmosphere in Hawai'i's
Hole-in-the-Wall Restaurants

David B. Goldman

with a foreword by
Alan Wong

3565 Harding Avenue
Honolulu, Hawai'i 96816
phone: (808) 734-7159
fax: (808) 732-3627
e-mail: sales@besspress.com
http://www.besspress.com

Design: Carol Colbath
Cover photo by Douglas Peebles

Library of Congress Cataloging-in-Publication Data

Goldman, David B.
  Island grinds : good food, real value,
and local atmosphere in Hawaii's hole-
in-the-wall restaurants / David B. Goldman ;
foreword by Alan Wong.
          p. cm.
  Includes glossary.
  ISBN 1-57306-224-3
  1. Restaurants - Hawaii - Guidebooks.
I. Title.
TX907.3.H3G65 2004   647.959-dc21

© 2004 by Bess Press, Inc.

08 07 06 05 04   5 4 3 2 1

Printed in Korea

CONTENTS

★
Da Bes'

ISLAND OF O‘AHU

Downtown

Ala Moana

Chinatown

Kaka‘ako

Nu‘uanu

Pāwa‘a

University

Mānoa

McCully

Waikīkī to Hawaiʻi Kai

ʻĀina Haina

Hawaiʻi Kai

Kaimukī

Kapahulu

Waikīkī

Windward

Kailua

Kāneʻohe

Kalihi-Pālama

ISLAND OF MAUI

FOREWORD

I first met David Goldman a few years back when he came into my King Street restaurant and sat at the chef's counter. He loved watching the front "line" plate up the dishes and was fascinated as each plate came over the counter. Obviously, he was appreciating the aroma and presentation of each dish. When he wasn't eating what he ordered himself, he'd be asking questions about the dishes, ingredients, sauces, or what have you.

I recently ran into David at Side Street Inn near Ala Moana, where I sometimes go to meet, eat, and "talk story" with friends like Roy Yamaguchi (Roy's Restaurant) and Dean Okimoto (Nalo Farms). David's first question to me as we shook hands was "Where do you guys go to eat? I mean, not your own upscale gourmet places, but local spots, the down-home joints?"

He told me he was already into 53 of some 120 restaurants he was writing about for his new book called "Island Grinds." And he had a pretty good list, compiled from places he knew over the years and from recommendations of people he'd run into, ranging from the valet car attendant at a hotel or a seatmate on an Aloha Airlines flight to the cooks and waitresses at the restaurants where he had already visited and dined.

But I gave him a few of my own favorites, and we got to talking that evening, comparing which out-of-the-way, obscure restaurants he and I had been to. That brought me back to island cooking—to the island foods that I've integrated for years into my own menus. Much of my own favorite eating today is still the good, simple comfort foods that can be found in the unpublicized small eateries in Hawai'i.

Certainly not all of Hawai'i's small, fun eating places are in this book, but a lot of them are, and even though not every dish on every menu is mentioned, this book does give the reader some very special dishes.

Don't you think it would be fun to follow these pages down our island streets, around the corners, and into so many unexpected doors of our neighborhood dining establishments?

CHEF ALAN WONG

PREFACE

When I was ten years old there was a tiny, hole-in-the-wall storefront Japanese delicatessen called George's in downtown Honolulu, on Union Mall behind the old Kress variety store. In the afternoons after school I used to go into George's for a couple of *inari* sushi—two for thirty-five cents. The taste of that fresh, succulent sushi was my introduction to the real food of the islands.

Ever since, wherever I've been in the world, I've been convinced that the best really local food is found in places like George's—the small places, the out-of-the-way dives, the holes-in-the-wall, the joints. Don't get me wrong; no one can outdo me in appreciation of Hawai'i's high-end, gourmet food. There is nothing like dining on "Hawaiian regional cuisine" at the top of the food chain, at fine restaurants such as Honolulu's Alan Wong's or Roy's or Chef Mavro's—truly fabulous eating.

In my seventeen years as a freelance travel writer, and for several of those years a restaurant critic for the *Los Angeles Times*, I've enjoyed cuisines—gourmet, local, or regional, call them what you will—all over the world, from Seattle to Moscow, from Rio de Janeiro to Singapore.

But my heart—not to mention my palate—has always been with the real food, the comfort food, the "down-home" dishes you'll find in any city in the world. And no one can say America doesn't have its share. Just think of the bursting hot dogs at Katz's Delicatessen on New York's Lower East Side, the luscious po-boy sandwiches at Casamento's in New Orleans, the drippy ribs at Arthur Bryant's in Kansas City, or the succulent raw oysters at Swan Oyster Depot in San Francisco.

Still, it's Hawai'i that I think boasts the most exciting mixture of foods in the country. And talk about "regional," what's really more "regional" in the islands than what we call "Local Food"?

But although this book is very much about local flavors—and my own admittedly opinionated, subjective take on those flavors—it is not just about Local Food (which islanders also call "grinds"). It's about good eating—with plenty of character added—whether it's O'ahu's most famous hamburger (and I'll have some comments on that baby), a steaming *laulau,* a piece of mahimahi, or simply a

x

gooey, overflowing plate lunch. In the other forty-nine states, fast food may mean a drive-through, but in these islands, we're talking plate lunch. A handful of these good eats—and certainly some of the most interesting—are already in the guidebooks but shouldn't be left out here because hey, who says that just because a place is in a guidebook, for the whole world to find, it's not any good?

But really, I wouldn't read this if I were looking for a pizza joint, or a southwest grill, or a taco restaurant. If you want those, check the Mainland.

And, let me admit, my idea of heaven at a counter may be some-one else's epitome of mediocrity. Nothing's more subjective than our opinions about food.

This is a book based in neighborhoods because, mostly, it is in the neighborhoods of the islands that much of this best food is found. It's not in the hotels, or the chain restaurants—even if you allow for McDonald's Spam, egg, and rice breakfast platter.

Some of these restaurants advertise; some do not. Most of them are family run. Some still cater to the plantation worker, opening before dawn and closing about noon. One or two are nothing more than food trucks on the side of the road. Some are so ethnic that—even if our Pidgin is okay—we'll find something on the table in front of us that we didn't think we'd ordered. Some have names that every local—but only the most savvy tourist—knows. Others are known only as far as the next neighborhood, but people wait to get in and every neighbor swears by the place. In some, if you want to eat right there you're going to be sitting on the curb outside. A handful have just one particular dish that's worth going there for. Some have food that's only so-so, but the atmosphere of the neigh-borhood, the warm and welcoming manner of the people serving you, the 'ohana feeling of Hawai'i that you get the moment you walk in—these make being there worthwhile.

Most of this is pretty inexpensive food—dare I say "cheap"?—and it nearly always comes in copious portions. "Dainty" doesn't cut it in Hawai'i.

And if, in these pages, you sometimes sense, "this guy must really like this place, he must just love the menu, or the feeling—or maybe he's just crazy about one of their dishes," why, you're right. That's why a handful of these Island Grinds are called ★Da Bes'.

The wonderful ethnic mixture of culture and cuisine that has come together in these isolated Pacific islands produces a fabulous table: the rice the Chinese insisted on when they came here to work the plantations; no poi for them! Or the sweet malassadas and spicy sausages the Portuguese brought. And who could even imagine eating much in Hawai'i without the *shoyu* of Japan? What about the Koreans, who brought with them garlics and hot peppers? Or the Filipinos, with their Malaysian and Spanish flavors? And let's not forget, islanders eat thousands of cans of Spam every week.

But this variety, this exciting mixture, all followed the native foods of the Hawaiians themselves, integrating with the sticky, gooey poi islanders have eaten for centuries, with the roast pork and fish, coconut and seaweeds.

For today's island resident, and for many visitors, food is not just a way of getting by in the world; it's an adventure, one we enjoy meal-to-meal. Because whether it's a plate lunch in Kalihi, a *manapua* snack from a Foodland market in Kapahulu, or a steak next to the beach in Kailua, Hawai'i's foods truly are unique.

Acknowledgments

To all of you who've helped me eat, who've sat with me on comfortable chairs and on dirty curbs, who've loved the food and hated it, who've argued with me—vehemently sometimes—about a dish, or a restaurant. To Shan, who's had to endure all those carbohydrates, to daughters Wendy and Pamela, who seemed to get more than their share of joints that didn't make the cut. To Joan Namkoong, for her expertise in defining some of the more esoteric dishes for me. To Wanda Adams, who often knew places I hadn't heard of. And to dozens of you whom I've met just briefly, but who steered me to your own favorite dives, joints, and holes-in-the-wall.

DAVID GOLDMAN'S FAVORITE DISHES AND WHERE TO EAT THEM

Portuguese bean soup: the only real meal, and a rich one it is, at Agnes' Portuguese Bake shop in Kailua, O'ahu.

taro burger: Aloha Aina Cafe in Wai'anae can get "sprouty," but the crispy sandwich entices me.

barbecued beef ribs: fat, gooey, and falling off the bone at Bob's Bar-B-Que in Kapālama.

banana pancakes with macadamia nut sauce: at Boots & Kimo's; just by itself this plate lures me to Kailua, O'ahu.

roast duck *manapua:* full and moist at Chun Wah Kam in Waimalu.

shrimp *sarciada:* great flavors and succulent shellfish at Elena's in Waipahu.

macaroni salad: it's a close call, but I'll have to go with the creamy version that Fukuya's in Mō'ili'ili dishes out.

bi bim bap: a big dish with big flavors at Gina's Bar-B-Q in Kaiumkī.

pork-stuffed eggplant: for me, Golden Palace Seafood Restaurant in Chinatown outdoes the competition with their juicy, melt-in-your-mouth dish.

fried rice: jammed with green onions, ham, and egg, it's an awfully common dish in the Islands, but I like Hukilau Cafe's in Lā'ie best.

karei karaage: yes, you eat the whole crispy fish, head, bones, and all, a big favorite for us crunch lovers at Izakaya Nonbei in Kapahulu.

corned beef hash: Junie's in Kāne'ohe has got to be the best—maybe it's the garlic.

Hawaiian sweet bread French toast: so rich, so flavorful, the dish at Kaka'ako Kitchen in Kaka'ako needs neither butter nor syrup.

french fries: Kua Aina in Hale'iwa may be famed for its hamburgers, but as far as I'm concerned it's the crisp, skinny French fries with the skins on that mark the place.

chop steak and onions: maybe it's the sirloin they use, but for me, whatever it is, Debbie Leong puts out the best chop steak in town.

loco moco: lots of mushrooms, gravy, and fried onions in this one, with their own homemade hamburger at Karen's Kitchen in Kaka'ako.

coco puff: there's not much competition in this field, but even if there were, Liliha Bakery and Coffee Shop in Liliha would be at the top with this luscious sweet.

beef with garlic and chili: slightly sweet, melts in your mouth, wonderful at Little Village Noodle House in Chinatown.

chives with egg casserole: sizzling appetizer dish served in the pan at the Kapahulu bistro called Mr. Ojisan.

warabaa: with sweet pickles and stew or curry sauce, this major version of loco moco is served at Liliha's New Uptown Fountain.

laulau: this is one case where the public is definitely right; the Hawaiian classic at Ono Hawaiian foods in Kapahulu is rightfully at the top of the heap.

tripe stew: granted, it's not a dish for everyone, but for those of us who enjoy it, Ono Loa at Waiāhole dishes out the best on the island.

barbecue teriyaki pork sandwich: soft, doughy bread soaked with meaty juices, plus lots of lettuce and gobs of mayonnaise, at Rainbow Drive In in Kapahulu.

pan-fried pork chops: great seasonings and the perfect place to enjoy them at Side Street Inn in Ala Moana.

Spicy Japanese clams: hidden among the displays of *poke*, this is a dish I don't think I've found anyplace else in the islands, certainly none as good as at Tanioka's in Waipahu.

chocolate *haupia* cream pie: I regularly need a fix of the not-too-sweet pastry for which Ted's Bakery at Sunset Beach is famous.

phô: you can argue from one end of the island to the other, but this broth, pure and rich, sets the standard, at Tochau in Chinatown.

stuffed mahimahi: at Yuki's in Pālama they stuff the fish with crab and vegetables, bake it, and layer it with cream sauce; I love it.

puka dog: just the best hot dog you'll find in the islands, maybe the best in the country, at Puka Dog in Po'ipū on Kaua'i.

salt and pepper squid: chewy, crisp and spicy, with hints of garlic, that's the squid at Hilo Rice Noodle in Hilo.

pūlehu: in oil, pepper, Hawaiian salt, and crisp garlic, the chicken or beef at Paul Muranaka's in Kona is to die for.

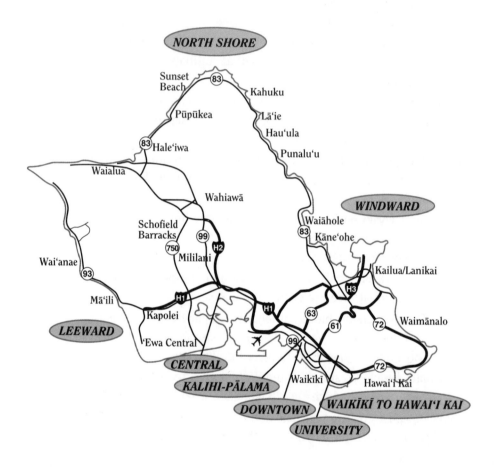

ISLAND OF
OʻAHU

Downtown
Ala Moana
Chinatown
Kakaʻako
Nuʻuanu
Pāwaʻa

University
Mānoa
McCully
Mōʻiliʻili

Waikīkī to Hawaiʻi Kai
ʻĀina Haina
Hawaiʻi Kai
Kaimukī
Kapahulu
Waikīkī

Windward
Kailua
Kāneʻohe
Lanikai
Waiāhole
Waimānalo

North Shore
Haleʻiwa
Kahuku
Lāʻie
Punaluʻu
Pūpūkea
Sunset Beach
Waialua

Central
ʻAiea
Mililani
Salt Lake
Wahiawā
Waimalu
Waipahu

Kalihi-Pālama
Kalihi
Kapālama
Liliha
Pālama
Sand Island

Leeward
ʻEwa Central
Kapolei
Māʻili
Waiʻanae

1

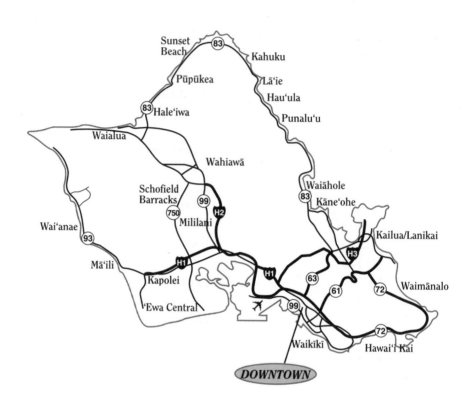

DOWNTOWN

Ala Moana
Green Papaya
Side Street Inn

Chinatown
Golden Palace Seafood Restaurant
Little Village Noodle House
Mabuhay Cafe & Restaurant
Mini Garden Noodle House
Royal Kitchen
Tochau
Urumi Noodle Cafe

Kakaʻako
George's Delicatessen
Kakaʻako Kitchen
Karen's Kitchen
Tropic Diner
Yanagi Sushi

Nuʻuanu
Bangkok Chef

Pāwaʻa
Champion Malasadas

GREEN PAPAYA

629 Keʻeaumoku St. • 953-2340
Monday–Saturday 10:30 a.m.-10 p.m., Sunday 11 a.m.-9 p.m.
BYOB? Yes • Credit cards? Yes
per person: $8-$14

Vietnam spreads all over the menu at this brightly lit, yet somehow soft room behind the corner at Keʻeaumoku and Makaloa Streets just up from Ala Moana. But this is no *phô* joint, nor does the cuisine stop at Vietnam. Thai specialties jump out from the menu pages, and traces of a local Hawaiʻi hide between the lines in dishes that show us "local" doesn't necessarily mean heavy, although portions are substantial. Flavors are pungent and mixed, but do not—repeat—do not, get carried away by what can be fiery chile spicing. Let Heidi Trang, who, with husband Bill in the kitchen, runs the place, or any other waitress be a guide to the fire on the plate. The Trangs also run another Green Papaya on the other side of downtown. Both spots feature dishes like spicy lemongrass chicken laced with garlic—tomato and cucumber on the side to cut the heat—or *phad thai,* or the house special vegetarian (lots of vegetarian dishes on this menu): a saucy heap of stir-fried snow peas, asparagus, tofu, and whatever other vegetable is handy that day. *Phô* has become one of the most popular dishes, and so have garden rolls stuffed with tofu, vegetables, and greens, with peanut sauce. Would you believe, even to those of us who think dessert is something that has to stick to the roof of your mouth, that the hot papaya tapioca is worth another helping? And have you ever tried salted lemonade?

Bottom Line: Spicy but light Southeast Asian flavors in a quiet, comfortable setting.

SIDE STREET INN

1225 Hopaka St. • 591-0253
Monday–Friday 10:30 a.m.-2:00 p.m., daily 4 p.m-1 a.m
BYOB? No, full bar • Credit cards? Yes
per person: $7-$15

What can you say about a place that's hard to find—just off Kapiʻolani Boulevard near Ala Moana—that's part knock 'em back bar, part karaoke and electronic darts, and has a menu from which you desperately want to order one of each? What you can say is that if you're sitting at the bar, whether eating or drinking, you're likely to find yourself in conversation with big time Hawaiian chefs, like Roy Yamaguchi or Alan Wong, who are regulars themselves. Sure, the several rooms are just a little shabby, but there's nothing shabby about the warm, professional service or the quality of the food. Who would have guessed it thirteen years ago when Colin Nishida opened up in the obscure location and began dishing out his pan-fried island pork chops and vegetable, *kamaboko* and sausage-filled fried rice (slightly crisp), both of which have become famous? "That's what made us," says Nishida, speaking of the oh-so-good chops that are seasoned and cooked perfectly, just like a sizzling platter of Spencer steak with sautéed onions and mushrooms, or even just the sandwiches and Buffalo fries. Maybe it helps that you can get half orders of many of the menu items, or that smoking is allowed, or that the bar boasts a good selection of draft beers. Just as good, salad greens are from Waimānalo's Nalo Farms, and the menu is interesting enough to feature dishes ranging from pan-fried ʻahi belly to breaded fried chicken gizzards, all just delicious.

Bottom Line: How can you beat lots of fun and great food in a let's-get-down-to-it joint?

GOLDEN PALACE SEAFOOD RESTAURANT

111 N. King St. • 521-8268
daily 7 a.m.-10 p.m.
BYOB? No • Credit cards? Yes
per person: $5-$8

The adventure of dining on dim sum is one of the few Hawaiian eating fests in which timing means something. If you show up too early, the full variety of dishes isn't yet making its way around the room. Too late, like midafternoon, and they've run out of half of the best items. But the midmorning regulars at Howard Lam's Golden Palace, on King Street next to the Bank of Hawaii in Chinatown, don't care. They're there just after ten in the morning when the place opens, older people at single tables, some hunched over Chinese language newspapers, quietly enjoying the morning's early dishes. Me, I think just before noon is the best time, even if sometimes you have to wait for a table, standing in the entryway next to the takeout station. Inside, the large dining room is decorated with Chinese art, pink tablecloths, and dark bamboo furniture. There is a large regular menu, but I prefer the carts of dim sum and their especially friendly, helpful servers, and I've noticed that here even the Chinese are not too shy to stand up and investigate the contents of the small bamboo steamer boxes on the carts, looking for a special delicacy. The pan-fried pork-stuffed eggplant is the best for blocks around, and I do love the steamed bean curd roll, not to mention steamed pork with bean curd, or deep-fried seaweed roll with shrimp, and I like the steamed seafood roll, even if the crab isn't crab.

Bottom Line: Relatively new, but coming into its own as one of Chinatown's most flavorful dim sum values.

LITTLE VILLAGE NOODLE HOUSE

★
Da Bes'

1113 Smith St. • 545-3008
Sunday–Thursday 10:30 a.m.-10:30 p.m.
Friday–Saturday 10:30 a.m.-12 p.m.
BYOB? Yes • Credit cards? Yes
per person: $5-$10

Two things invariably strike me as I walk out the door at Little Village, rubbing my stomach, sighing with satisfaction, and belching: it's hard to go wrong with nearly anything on the menu, and this isn't really a noodle shop. The restaurant Jennifer Chan opened three years ago hosts a multiregional bill of fare, primarily Northern China and Cantonese, and although the light, blond wooden furniture and simple decor probably aren't going to be featured in *Architectural Digest* magazine, neither is it the grubby hole you might expect in its location, just *mauka* of Hotel Street. To avoid confusion and simplify dealing with the broad menu, try discussing its offerings with the waiters, who are articulate and attentive. They'll have brought tea as soon as you're seated, so you're already getting into the swing of things while ordering. Among a multitude of good choices: pan-fried beef with garlic and chili is delicious, breaded and cooked in a slightly sweet sauce, the beef bites melting in your mouth; pot stickers are among the best in town, and certainly one of the best values on the menu, eight large, bursting dumplings, like chicken and chive and, get this, they're cooked in olive oil; dried green beans with ground pork and a mild dose of chiles, firm and refreshing. And, just to calm things down, a quiet, fulfilling plate of Shanghai noodles, thick and round, with black fungus, pork, Chinese cabbage and green onions. All this and—in Chinatown yet—there's parking in the rear.

Bottom Line: Some of Chinatown's very best eating, with service to match. Might even need reservations.

MABUHAY CAFE & RESTAURANT

1049 River St. • 545-1956
daily 10 a.m.-10 p.m.
BYOB? No, beer and wine served. • Credit cards? Yes
per person: $7-$10

Red-and-white-checkered oil cloths on the tables, a serious and extensive menu of homestyle Filipino cooking and a handful of old local guys sitting at stools drinking coffee and talking sports—that pretty much tells the story at this Chinatown institution. Filomena and Carmelita Lumauag's restaurant has been around for forty years (at the present location just *mauka* of King Street for the last fifteen). Bustling through the L-shaped room in a mixture of Tagalog and American—although the Elvis Presley coming from the jukebox is pure Elvis English—the waitresses are busy most of the day and into the evening carrying plates out of the kitchen filled with some of the island's best—and certainly most interesting—Filipino food. There are the basics: rich *pansit*, heavy and moist with vegetables and meat morsels; meaty pork adobo simmering in its garlic and vinegar; and *lumpia*, either banana or vegetable. Then they've got the more interesting dishes: pork *pinacbet*, loaded with bittermelon, eggplant, and long beans stewed in broth and fish sauce; *kilawen* shrimp, reeking with the flavors of the 7,000-island archipelago: *shoyu*, ginger, and garlic. You usually get a choice of fish when ordering fish *sarciado* (watch out for the bony monkfish), the fillet pan-fried and served in a sauce of garlic, onions, tomato, and seasonings. One caveat for the *haole:* it just may be that some of the dishes come toned down if you've got light skin, since although I've heard the word "bland" from an occasional Anglo, we haven't heard it from our Filipino friends.

Bottom Line: Lots to choose from in good dishes at this leading Filipino restaurant.

8

MINI GARDEN NOODLE HOUSE

50 N. Hotel St. • 538-1273
daily 10:30 a.m.-11:30 p.m.
BYOB? No • Credit cards? Yes
per person: $4-$6

Noodles love Chinatown's corners—Japanese, Vietnamese, Chinese, noodles wherever you look, and the intersection of Hotel and Smith Streets is no exception. Don't let the name of the place fool you. There's no garden anywhere near, but inside it's nowhere near as grubby as these places can be. Several years ago the owners took what had been a dingy, fading store and redid it. Congratulations, guys, because today the thirty-one-year-old establishment is well-lit, light and airy, and an interesting array of passing foot traffic is well visible through large windows—as are the thundering Hotel Street buses, which sometimes seem to be running right alongside your table. The Cantonese fare covers the usual gamet of appetizers, noodles, rice, and soups. And if in Hawai'i shave ice after noodles isn't incongruous, the smoothies here certainly are. Plus, there's a decent selection of pearl cream and bubble teas. But forget the sidelines, what you want here is noodles, although one exception to that rule would be a hot, comforting bowl of very nice *congee* (with pork giblets and preserved egg, if you're feeling adventurous). Otherwise, stewed noodles with *char siu* and *choy sum* is one of the tastiest dishes on the menu, and stewed duck leg noodle is served in a delicious broth, its large, meaty duck leg and thigh making an exceptionally satisfying meal. At night, the area is still just a little iffy, but that doesn't seem to stop young couples with children, women by themselves, or oldsters slipping in for a bowl.

Bottom Line: Good people-watching with a high quality-to-value ratio in stewed noodle.

ROYAL KITCHEN

Let's listen up here and pay attention. On their business cards, the four partners who've owned this slightly-out-of-the-ordinary dim sum place since 1974 are trying to tell us something: "Home of the Baked Manapua." And yep, baked *manapua* is what they do best. When you walk into the small, open-front store facing the pedestrian mall just *makai* of Kukui and River Streets on the edge of Chinatown, you'll see shelves of baked dim sum—Portuguese sausage, *lup cheong,* curried chicken, vegetables, *char siu, kālua* pork, and more. Those who've been stuck on steamed *manapua* just may find themselves converted; this is good stuff. They also have the steamed variety, plus a pretty fair pork hash and some undistinguished half moons, but baked *manapua* is the way to go. There are a couple of other interesting dishes: ti leaf–wrapped *joong* is heavy and tasty, its *mochi* rice wrapped around duck egg and roast pork. By itself, the *char siu* is flavorful and tender, and more than once I've awkwardly fumbled my chopsticks through an appetizing plate of braised pig's feet. Since this is purely a food stand restaurant without its own indoor seating, customers walk outside to the edge of the stream, where there are concrete tables and seating under cover. And let's face it, this is a "maybe" zone: earlier in the day the crowd is more elderly, some playing checkers on built-in checkerboards, but around noon it seems to change and the crowd lounging around gets younger, shall we say a bit rowdier? But not enough to keep us away from the baked *manapua.*

Bottom Line: Interesting little place to eat excellent baked *manapua* with an intriguing mix of fellow citizens.

TOCHAU

1007 River St. • 533-4549
daily 8 a.m.-2:30 p.m.
BYOB? Yes • Credit cards? No
per person: $4-$8

It's as good as the line outside says, and there nearly always is a line waiting for the steaming-hot bowls of classic Vietnamese *phô* served in an old, stone-fronted building on the edge of Chinatown just steps *mauka* of King Street. You'd think the restaurant had been there forever, but in fact it's only been about sixteen years that Hoac and John To have been running it, filling the high-ceilinged, linoleum-floored sixty-seat room every day with mostly Asian faces, plus a sprinkling of haoles. If you're by yourself in that line, here's a secret: the host, or hostess (who doesn't always have much English), can frequently put you at a common eating table. The menu does have a handful of rice noodle dishes, and a couple of appetizers, but perhaps these are best avoided. The clear beef broth is just about the richest in town, laden with choices of meats—rare steak, tripe, tendon, or brisket—and mixed with handfuls of fresh greens and sprouts brought to the table, or more strongly flavored with a choice of bottled sauces—plum, fish, or spicy, even *shoyu*. The drink of choice here: plastic glasses of pale tea. Don't bother asking for the bill; just walk up to the counter and they'll dig it out for you.

Bottom Line: It's worth the wait for one of the best—if not *the* best bowls of soup in town.

Urumi Noodle Cafe

142 N. King St.• 531-8446
daily 8 a.m.-11 p.m.
BYOB? Yes • Credit cards? No
per person: $4-$6

One humid afternoon when the trades were down, Chinatown was sweltering, and I was feeling ravenous, I walked into Urumi Noodle, sat down, and ordered three times more than I'd probably be able to eat at the table. My waitress, as she scribbled in her order pad, looked up and shook her head. "Too much," she said, "too much." Right she was, but sometimes, who cares? Especially at a neat little spot like this, which has been in this corner location on Kekaulike Mall for nearly five years and where the prices are so low. Often you have to share a table, and since the Oʻahu Market is right across the street, fellow diners at the eight Formica tables frequently crowd the floor under their seats with shopping bags full of vegetables, fish, and meats, enjoying an after-shopping meal, widely gesturing with their chopsticks, and chatting in a language that is not English. The waitress is right, of course. Each dish is a meal in itself, whether it's the Thousand Year Egg with lean pork, pork liver, or a bowl of *ramen*. Consider fish cake *look fun*: a large bowl of broth laden with chewy fish cake, noodles, and *choy sum*; or minute chicken cake noodle: a big plate that could use a dose of hot sauce but that's loaded with cake noodle, chicken, and *choy sum*. One exceptional choice? Curry *ramen*. You can smell the curry coming from across the room, a slightly thickened broth with noodles, bean sprouts, pork, fish cake, green onions, and beef. Yum.

Bottom Line: An honest noodle shop giving good value in the heart of the city.

GEORGE'S DELICATESSEN

1317 S. Beretania St. • 597-8069
Monday–Saturday 9 a.m.-3 p.m.
BYOB? No • Credit cards? No
per person: $3-$5

Remember when you were a kid and ate something for the very first time and loved it, and never forgot it? That's me and George's. The little *okazuya* has moved from the original downtown location where I first paid $.35 for two *inari* sushi over fifty years ago, and today the Ueda family, which took over in 1956, is always either at the front or busy in the kitchen, but it still looks the same to me when I walk in the door. I don't recall that there were people waiting to get in when they opened in those earlier days, or that there was a constant stream of customers walking out the door carrying large orders in cut-down cardboard boxes as there is today. But I still want to order one—maybe two—of each of the appetizing items displayed behind the glass food cases, and the dish of choice in today's George's is still sushi. I like the large *inari* and a *maki* roll. Then I want a helping of *chow fun*, and a piece of deep-fried boneless chicken, or a hash patty that's very potatoey but has an addictive, peppery tang to it. And while I'm waiting—or chowing down at one of the two small tables—a lot of plate lunches go out the door: fried fish, barbecue chicken and teriyaki beef, and plenty of bentos, the most popular small one stuffed with Spam and egg, barbecue beef and chicken, rice and chow mein.

Bottom Line: Who says you can't go home again, if home is a small *okazuya* that's been serving good *inari* and *maki* sushi for over fifty years?

KAKAʻAKO KITCHEN

1200 Ala Moana Blvd. • 596-7488
Monday–Thursday 7 a.m.-9 p.m., Friday–Saturday 7 a.m.-10 p.m.
Sunday 7 a.m.-5 p.m.
per person: $5-$9

Call it what you will: "sophisticated," "healthy," "adventurous," even "gourmet." Whatever the word, it's got to be Oʻahu's most upscale plate lunch. Sure, it's served on the usual Styrofoam plates, the cutlery is plastic, the floor's concrete, and the plastic and wooden tables, either inside or outside under roof, are sticky. But after you order at the counter they actually bring it to the table when the food's ready. The food itself? Some of the best dishes on the island, with a flair that would set them apart even if the "uptown" location in Ward Centre at the corner of Auahi and Kamakeʻe, or the prices, didn't already do that. Russell Siu, whose pricy 3660 on the Rise restaurant is considered one of the best in the city, has carried that quality over into his own local food joint. Perhaps some dishes, like the homemade corned beef hash, aren't especially distinctive, but a sister breakfast plate, Hawaiian egg bread French toast, is so rich, so delicious it doesn't even need syrup. And there's that moist, scrumptious banana/poi bread, or Siu's own roast coffee—you coffee drinkers will love it. The pastries are great, like chocolate brownies or an especially creamy bread pudding topped with vanilla bean sauce. Pan-seared Aloha tofu burger is one of a handful of purportedly healthier entrées, but I go crazy over what they call Island-style chicken linguini, with grilled eggplant, mushrooms, and sun-dried tomatoes, all pulled together in a unique hoisin cream sauce. Not to mention plenty of salads, an interesting list of sandwiches, and a small but good list of draft beers.

Bottom Line: A classy selection of plate lunches, salads, sandwiches, and desserts.

KAREN'S KITCHEN

614 Cooke St. • 597-8195
Monday–Friday 5:30 a.m.-9 p.m., Saturday 5:30 a.m.-4 p.m.
BYOB? Yes • Credit cards? No
per person: $3-$9

Karen Yamaoka puts out a great loco moco. She does some other tummy-fillers gratifyingly well too, from the Kitchen she's run for eleven years in the light industrial area of Kaka'ako, at the Ilaniwai intersection. While they're waiting, her regulars head for the television set, usually tuned to a news channel, in a far corner, while in her clean-cut, roomy restaurant, the friendly staff, dressed in bright yellow "Karen's Kitchen" tee-shirts, takes orders, hands platters of food across the counter, and carries overflowing plates to the tables. But back to the loco moco. It's a large, impressive dish, beautiful to look at. I think the secret to its success is the hamburger patty, made on the premises and cooked crisply. It tastes like it's homemade: plenty of mushrooms in the gravy and lots of fried onions around the patty. Did I say the bill of fare was eclectic? How about corned beef and cabbage? And an appetizing bacon, lettuce, and tomato sandwich with crisp bacon and plenty of lettuce, tomato, and mayonnaise on soft, fresh bread. On the counter are pieces of homemade sheet cakes in chocolate and vanilla flavors, next to the *musubi,* its rice loaded with *furikake.* The restaurant also sells a lot of bentos. Regulars come in for Karen's steaks, like a 10-ounce rib-eye, or for the specialty foods: Hawaiian on Wednesdays, Filipino on Thursdays, and prime rib on Fridays.

Bottom Line: An up-to-date dining spot mixing local food with sheet cakes, and don't forget the loco moco.

ISLAND OF O'AHU • DOWNTOWN • KAKA'AKO

15

TROPIC DINER

1020 Auahi St.• 597-8429
Monday–Saturday 7 a.m.-2 p.m., Sunday 7 a.m.-12:30 p.m.
BYOB? No, full bar • Credit cards? Yes
per person: $5-$10

Budweiser beer signs and orange Naugahyde booths, television sets blaring in two corners, and "pretty good local food," swears the guy at the next booth, who's a five-mornings-a-week customer. A very good place for a guy to hang out, this is, at the Diamond Head end of the long green Ward Farmers Market building. When you walk in and look around, it feels like a bar, filled with local businessmen in aloha shirts, construction workers, and a handful of retirees. And there is a bar, although it's only a service bar at the back, with a small but surprisingly good selection of spirits and a good beer list. In fact, the bar and the beer list take over after two in the afternoon, when the regular menu disappears and drinks and pupus are the only things served—an interesting idea that Glenn Tanoue came up with when he opened the place in 1997. And do you know another breakfast plate that has sashimi, grilled *shoyu* *ahi*, miso soup, Spam, rice, and a green onion omelet—all together? Small amounts of each, but exceptionally nice morning dining. Everything they do with fish is good, as you'll begin to see if you try the garlic *ʻahi*. Another breakfast standout is *lup cheong* omelet, cooked thin and stuffed with a good quantity of shredded sausage; the crisp fried potatoes on the side are among the best on the island. Beef stew is another favorite, heavy and rich in its sauce, and homemade hamburger steak smothered with grilled onions that haven't been cooked to mush. Last but not least, in keeping with this male environment, a ten-ounce rib steak.

Bottom Line: Great idea in a combination of fine local food, good service, and a bar.

YANAGI SUSHI

762 Kapiʻolani Blvd.• 597-1525
daily 11:00 a.m.-2 p.m., Monday–Saturday 5:30 p.m.-2 a.m.
Sunday 5:30 p.m.-10 p.m.
BYOB? No, full bar • Credit cards? Yes
per person: $15-$30

It's okay that the menu has tempura and combination dinners and *nabemono* and teriyaki steaks and sashimi and barbecue beef and *tonkatsu* and comfortable tables at which to eat all of these. But the thing that's the most delicious at Yanagi Sushi is—what else?—sushi, and maybe some small plates of pupus out of the ocean. The Yanagi (Koreans, yet) family has been dishing it out at this Kapiʻolani location near Ward Avenue since 1978, and they've had to expand several times. The usually crowded restaurant is not exactly unknown, its walls plastered with photographs of local celebrities and nobodies. Actually, there are two sushi bars, one in front as you walk in and another behind that. The menu boasts a modest but good selection of sakes, western wines, spirits, and beers. Could it be these that enhance the usual camaraderie you find at sushi bars? Is that why the couple next to you is all over each other and while she has one arm around him, with chopsticks in the other hand she's forking *uni* into her mouth? The fish is as fresh as restaurant fish gets, which may be why perhaps it is the basics that are best. That *uni*, as someone two seats away says, is "like ambrosia." The broiled *anago* melts in your mouth. The sushi chef, it is true, can be a bit forgetful and has to be reminded again about an order of *geso yaki*—the broiled squid legs, which can be a little chewier than you'd like—but then again, a bowl of *toro tataki*—delicious tuna tartare—can make up for that.

Bottom Line: A fine place to enjoy the freshest in sushi. And—at just how many sushi bars will you find "reserved" signs?

BANGKOK CHEF

1627 Nuʻuanu Ave.• 585-8839
Monday–Saturday 10 a.m.-8 p.m.
BYOB? Yes • Credit cards? Yes
per person: $4-$7

If you're passing by, the open storefront still looks like the fruit and vegetable market Patrick and Sansane Chang started on Nuʻuanu Avenue three years ago. Parking out in front, *mauka* of School Street, is still for minicars (although there is some parking in the rear), and the piles of papayas, Japanese eggplant, pineapples, and apple bananas that originally made up the decor are still there. But they put in three tables when Sansane—Thai by birth—started cooking her native dishes in the back, and the produce displays shrank as more tables appeared, so you'd have to guess there's more money in hot Thai dishes than in cold papayas. The market's days may be numbered, but in the kitchen Sansane has a light—if uneven—touch, so here more than most places it's a good idea to know what to order. Pan-fried fish patties, of minced fish cake with long beans and kaffir lime leaves, need the special house sauce to neutralize their saltiness. But *phad thai* is a tasty dish, cooked with that same sauce, and chives are a nice touch. Green papaya salad is overwhelmed with garlic and its papaya tougher than you'd like, but chicken *laab*, eaten in cabbage leaves, combines texture and spices—shallots, mint leaves, dried chili peppers—to bring out the best in the traditional Southeast Asian dish. Best of all comes an excellent green curry chicken, rich with coconut milk and curry paste, eggplant and kaffir lime leaves, bamboo shoots and peas. And although the apple bananas may disappear from the shelves one day, they'll live on in dessert, deliciously simmered in hot coconut milk sweetened with palm sugar.

Bottom Line: The kitchen puts a nice touch on most of its dishes for easy Thai dining.

CHAMPION MALASADAS

1926 S. Beretania St. • 947-8778
Tuesday–Saturday 6 a.m.-9 p.m., Sunday 6:30 a.m.-7 p.m.
BYOB? No • Credit cards? No
per person: $1-$4

Awhile back the *Honolulu Advertiser* did an in-house tasting of some of the city's premier malassadas. Champion won, they say, but we also have to remind ourselves that the long-running Leonard's, not too far away, may have at least as good a product, and that food is always an especially subjective subject. Joc Miw, the Champion owner, did once work at Leonard's himself, so it's a close call. The doughnut-like pastry that the Portuguese contributed to Hawai'i's menu is, in this small store just 'Ewa of McCully Street, truly excellent. It's got to be eaten hot, or at least warm, right out of the oil, and if you eat on the premises, you're going to be either standing outside or sitting on one of the four chairs in the light, plain store, which also makes excellent cross buns. Your hands will be sticky from the yeasty, eggy dough and the crisp crust and its thin coating of granulated sugar, but inside your mouth these malassadas explode with goodness. There's also a small selection of Hawaiian breakfasts, with eggs and an assortment of meat choices, such as Portuguese sausage, Spam, and *lup cheong*. The store is busy all day, but watch out, especially around seven in the morning, when boxes of the sweet, hot morsels are carried out by the armful.

Bottom Line: Maybe the best malassada in the city, at the least a gooey, wonderful mouthful of flavor and texture.

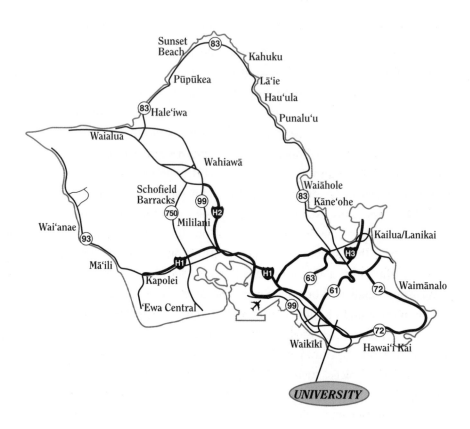

University

Mānoa
Manoa Bar-B-Q
Tatsu Japanese Restaurant

McCully
Hata Restaurant
Jimbo Restaurant
McCully Chop Suey

Mōʻiliʻili
Fukuya

Manoa Bar-B-Q

2752 Woodlawn Dr. • 988-4979
daily 9 a.m.-9 p.m.
BYOB? Yes • Credit cards? Yes
person: $4-$8

Give a pass to the breaded pork chops. Even in gravy they're awfully dry, although large and nicely breaded. But don't go away, because on a bill of fare with over three dozen plate lunch choices and nearly twenty sandwiches, you can still do pretty well at this small Mānoa Valley place tucked in with several other restaurants between the Safeway market and a Longs drugstore in Mānoa Marketplace. Even with the lengthy regular menu, sometimes the best dish is one of the specials, like fried noodles: a hefty portion of seasoned noodles packed with cabbage and chicken. The barbecue chicken, in several combination plates, may be the best plate lunch chicken in the valley (please, don't bother reminding me that there's not much competition for that honor). A surprise favorite? The chili dog plate: two hot dogs—and they aren't those anemic sausages we sometimes get—lathered in a sweet and tangy chile bean sauce, with plenty of ground meat and the usual scoops of rice and macaroni salad on the side. You can eat inside, under the T-bar ceiling at Formica tables or, preferably, enjoy the breeze coming down the valley at several small outside tables. Steven Chan, who has a couple of other restaurants on the island, does a good job in Mānoa.

Bottom Line: Easy eating with a selective handful of good dishes.

TATSU JAPANESE RESTAURANT

2908 E. Mānoa Rd. • 988-2134
Monday–Saturday 11 a.m.-1 p.m., 5 p.m.-9 p.m.
BYOB? Yes • Credit cards? No
per person: $7-$14

When they were decorating the place two years ago someone—maybe chef-owner Tatsuo Iisuka—must have stood at the door, looked at the white walls, frowned, and thrown a handful of framed Japanese prints into the air. Since the room's just nine feet wide, some hit the white walls and stuck. But customers don't seem to mind the lack of sophistication; as graduate students from the university or older Japanese living up in Mānoa, it's what they've come to appreciate in their neighborhood restaurant. And in the eighteen seats it's not surprising that diners often know one another. No Michelin stars here, but the Iisuka family, including wife and bushy-haired son who's often the room's waiter, give their clientele want they want: cozy simplicity in food and environment. It's no surprise to see a single diner hunched over his thesis in a corner of the room, even though that might seem more natural in a Starbucks, like the one four doors away. Here, sashimi and tempura are both popular, even though the sashimi isn't always Numbah One grade. Udon *unaga* is three fat, tender slabs of eel, *shoyu*-glazed over a bowl of rice, and the butterfish *misozuke* slides succulently over your palate. But in keeping with the homeyness of the restaurant, it's the broth dishes that provide the most satisfaction. *Kitsune* udon showcases the soup, hot and flavorsome with fish cake, noodles, greens, and bean curd, slightly sweetened with rice wine. An economical lunch menu features *teishoku* servings.

Bottom Line: Simple is the word for the menu, food, and atmosphere in a Japanese cafe.

HATA RESTAURANT

1742 S. King St. • 941-2686
daily except Sunday 10:30 a.m.-2:30 p.m, 5 p.m.-8:45 p.m.
BYOB? Yes • Credit cards? No
per person: $7-$10

When you push through the double doors into Hata Restaurant the first thought is that you've stumbled into someone's dining room by mistake and the whole family is there. The plain, high-ceilinged room has just eight tables, and the customers seem so at home that surely they must know one another. For thirty years the feeling, menu, and clientele in this very Japanese McCully store-front, across the street from a Zippy's, really have seemed like home to its customers. One guy comes five days a week to eat Yasuhiro Hata's food and be waited on by Hata's wife, Sakae. Not that the food is so great, served mostly in bowls and *teishoku* boxes between walls graced by colorful flower photos (they're for sale) and sumo posters (they're not). But it is simple and well pre-pared—let's call it your basic Japanese comfort food. A *teishoku* menu is available, but it's the single menu dishes—each served with *tsukemono*, miso soup, rice, and tea in lovely *teishoku* boxes—or one of the specials tacked up on a bulletin board on the wall, that seem the most popular. The tempura dishes are good, but the more interesting plates include sweet and flaky *misosuke ʻahi* belly, or deep-fried oysters dipped in *ponzu* sauce. Noodle dishes come so hot you've got to wait awhile to begin slurping; one of these favorites is *oyako* udon, filled to the brim with a savory broth, Spanish onions, chicken, green onions, chicken, bamboo shoots, and egg. It all goes pretty well with the Japanese music in the back-ground.

Bottom Line: A cozy, longtime neighborhood restaurant with com-fortable food.

24

JIMBO RESTAURANT

1936 King St. • 947-2211
daily 11 a.m.-3 p.m., 5 p.m.-10 p.m.
BYOB? Yes • Credit cards? Yes
per person: $6-$10

On the sidewalk outside there's usually a line for those who have already signed their names on the clipboard hanging on the plate glass window. Inside, most of the customers in the open room, obviously locals, in tee shirts and shorts, are slurping from large ceramic bowls filled with noodles and broth. On King Street in a small strip mall next to King's Cafe, Naoki and Mikiki Motojima have been running the real thing in a Japanese noodle house since they opened the place some ten years ago. At first glance, the menu in the bamboo-ceilinged room, which seats maybe sixty diners, looks pretty extensive, but make no mistake, even though it lists *donburi* and rice curries, noodles are the thing here. They make their own, both udon and soba, served either hot or cold (there's an extra charge for "skinny" noodles). A good choice is the "ten-don combo," which lets you choose shrimp tempura, vegetables, or *kakiage,* and comes with a side bowl of udon. The shrimp are firmly tender, with a crunchy tempura batter that makes the dish especially delicious. In a little more exotic vein is the *ume wakame*, the udon noodles in a hot broth with seaweed and salted plum. Side dishes themselves run the gamut: seaweed, tempura chips, or just a simple fried egg. Sometimes, as we know, noodle broths can stand to be jazzed up a bit, so don't be afraid to sprinkle a little red pepper mix in, or a dash of *shoyu.*

Bottom Line: Beautiful flavors in a real local noodle house.

McCully Chop Suey

2005 S. King St. • 946-4069
Sunday–Wednesday 10 a.m.-10 p.m.
Thursday–Saturday 10 a.m.-11 p.m.
BYOB? Yes • Credit cards? Yes
per person: $6-$9

It's Saturday night and a bunch of local Japanese in their twenties troop in and seat themselves at a large round table in the center of the high-ceilinged dining room. A waitress hustles out of the kitchen carrying hot platters of Peking duck and buns and begins dishing out. I don't know whether this is a ritual, but it's only the first of the evening's dishes for this cheery party in that building we've all driven by for years at the corner of King Street and McCully. It seems as though the restaurant with the big bright red, green, and blue neon has been there forever. But in this case forever is 1957, and at that it's been through four owners. Still, at least two of Honolulu's most prestigious nearby restaurants regularly send over for takeout from the huge menu. At first, you might wonder why, but then, as you dig in to your order, the subtleties of the Cantonese flavoring come out and the tastes become more distinct. The bill of fare actually has only a handful of chop suey dishes, but dozens of other *mein* plates. The most popular items are fairly conventional: sweet-and-sour spareribs in the usual large local portions, crispy *gau gee mein* with noodles, vegetables, *char siu,* fried pork, and seafood. Two of the menu's stand-out dishes? Fillets of steamed fish—usually flounder—served butter-tender in a sauce of ginger and green onions, and tripe with vegetables, simmering in a rich black bean sauce.

Bottom Line: Long-established Honolulu chop suey restaurant serving flavorful, dependable food that's by no means all chop suey.

FUKUYA

2710 S. King St. • 946-2073
Wednesday–Sunday 6 a.m.-2 p.m.
BYOB? No • Credit cards? Yes
per person: $3-$5

On Fridays, Saturdays, and Sundays the line often snakes out the door, and customers have to park down the block while they run in to pick up selections of their favorite goodies. You may even have to actually take a number! The Fukuya name has run an *okazuya* in the Mō'ili'ili neighborhood for more than fifty years, but today's incarnation, across the street from a Sherwin-Williams paint store, still has a plain white interior and clean glass food display cases—with identifying labels on the food platters, yet!—and may be the most popular ever. If you're lucky, while you're waiting you can camp at the one small table with three chairs and watch the action while hoping they won't run out of the dish you want before it's your turn to order. Rich tofu cakes, luscious creamy macaroni salad that may just set the standard for the city, hefty slabs of sweet potato tempura, good *inari* sushi in large and small sizes, and great teriyaki meatballs. The crab cakes are pretty popular, but even some longtime customers admit they tend to get a little salty, and you could say the same for the tofu fish burgers. All this, and they make their own cookies?

Bottom Line: Good selection of some of the best takeout in town, and don't forget the macaroni salad.

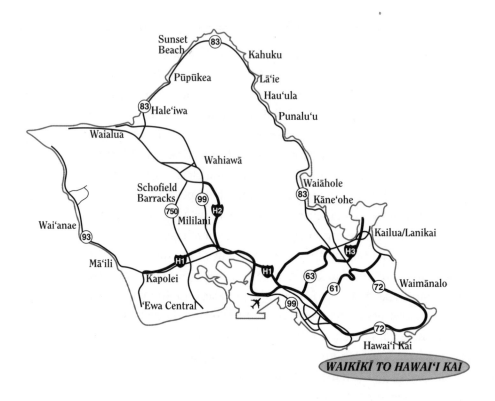

WAIKĪKĪ TO HAWAIʻI KAI

WAIKĪKĪ TO HAWAIʻI KAI

ʻĀina Haina
Jack's Restaurant

Hawaiʻi Kai
Thai Valley Cuisine

Kaimukī
Gina's Bar-B-Que
Kwong On
Sekiya's Restaurant & Delicatessen

Kapahulu
Izakaya Nonbei
Leonard's Bakery
Mr. Ojisan
Ono Hawaiian Foods
Rainbow Drive In
Sunrise Restaurant
Tokkuri Tei

Waikīkī
Eggs 'N Things
Phô Tri

JACK'S RESTAURANT

820 W. Hind Dr. • 373-4034
daily 6 a.m.-2 p.m.
BYOB? No • Credit cards? Yes
per person: $6-$8

For breakfast at Jack's the dish is fish fillet with eggs, but with a caveat: unless you read the small print on the menu, the four small fillets covered with chopped green onions show up on the plate breaded in flour and egg and then fried. Better to order "Hawaiian style," with rock salt, garlic, and pepper. That, regulars insist, is the way to order the dish. And that's the way they've been doing it for nearly forty years at Jack's in the ʻĀina Haina Shopping Center on Kalanianaʻole Highway almost to Hawaiʻi Kai. The room, which seats maybe four dozen, is decorated with ceiling fans and plenty of white latticework. For the last five years Michele Lee and husband Norman have been the owners, serving both breakfast and lunch, but where the emphasis is—as the morning crowds on weekends make plain—is clearly breakfast. Lunch is mostly sandwiches and daily specials like lamb curry, *kālua* roast turkey, and Jack's Special fried rice (not a bad dish, filled with green onions and egg and ham). Breakfast is the time for that fish fillet, or a large portion of corned beef hash—so potatoey that it's a particularly good example of why corned beef hash as usually served in the islands may not be Hawaiʻi's finest contribution to the culinary arts. The hamburger steak with eggs is another of the restaurant's most popular dishes, floating in gravy and topped with fresh onions lightly fried.

Bottom Line: Popular local breakfast and lunch spot, easily accessible to nearby middle-class neighborhoods.

THAI VALLEY CUISINE

501 Kealahou St. • 395-9746
daily 4 p.m.-9 p.m.
BYOB? Yes • Credit cards? Yes
per person: $7-$10

To say you're not likely to just stumble across this out-of-the-way eatery would be an understatement. The Kalama Valley Shopping Center, in a residential area at the rear of Hawai'i Kai, is a retail disaster, a virtual ghost town, the Thai restaurant one of only two tenants. But Carole Thirakoun, who started the place with a partner whom she later bought out, has stuck it out for twelve years. Today, she's working the stoves almost every evening for a mostly local clientele from the surrounding neighborhood. The neighbors know the drill: most bring their own beer or wine; the waitress opens it and brings out chilled glasses. The window curtains in the room are lace, the tables decorated with white linen tablecloths and pink napkins, and Thai music in the background struggles with noises from a bustling open kitchen. Crispy calamari is one of the most asked-for appetizers, very heavily breaded, and another breaded dish, crispy fish fillet—most often red snapper—is equally popular, although the fish occasionally tends to be mushy. Red curry, with chicken, beef, or pork, is adorned with eggplant, bamboo shoots, and basil—one of the best dishes on the menu. Even when the curries are ordered hot, you needn't worry about blowing out the insides of your mouth, but if you're still steaming, *phad thai* can be the neutralizing dish that eases the fires.

Bottom Line: Nothing exciting, but it goes down well as a comfortable, attractive dinner stop if you live in Hawai'i Kai, or on the way home from Sandy Beach.

GINA'S BAR-B-QUE

2919 Kapi'olani Blvd. • 735-7964
Sunday–Thursday 10 a.m.-10 p.m.
Friday–Saturday 10 a.m.-11 p.m.
BYOB? Yes • Credit cards? No
per person $4-$8

The food the two sisters who run Gina's dish out tastes as good as it looks; you know by looking at it that you're in for a good meal. Granted that most of us have frequently been dazzled—and disillusioned—at other places by how the food looks on display, at Gina's there won't be any of those nasty surprises. What you see is what you get, and what you get is simply good food. Gina Song and Yong Han, who've been cooking for some fourteen years there close to the Foodland Market in Market City Shopping Center, know what they're doing with Korean food. Studying the menu in their small, well-lit store with gray linoleum tiles on the floor, a couple of tables and a handful of counter stools, you'll probably realize this is more than a conventional Korean barbecue. Yes, the *kal bi* is okay, and so are the barbecued meats and chicken. But *bi bim bap* is a truly gutsy dish: mixing together its rice, beef, vegetables, sauce, and egg can put you away for the day. Simple dishes, such as lightly breaded squash *jun* or *man doo*, are well prepared, but really it's in the spicy dishes that the kitchen seems to come most alive. Spicy pork can make your taste buds want to fall in love, and the *yook kae jang* is so rich in flavors and spices you almost want to dive into it. The choices in vegetables change daily. Sang, who is Yong Han's son and the manager, has it right when he says, "We know most of our clients." It's easy to see why.

Bottom Line: Better than most Korean restaurants, it's more than a Korean barbecue.

KWONG ON

3620 Wai'alae Ave. • 734-4666
Monday–Saturday 7:30 a.m.-3 p.m.
BYOB? No • Credit cards? No
per person: $3-$5

Timing is everything. That's why, even if they do open at 7:30 in the morning, it's best not to show up at this takeout spot in downtown Kaimukī until after nine, when the whole inventory of yummy dishes prepared back in the kitchen has been brought up front for sale and everything in the display cases is warm and fresh. Be careful you're not knocked down by someone hurrying out the front door with a large bag of goodies, on his way to office, home, or picnic. But there's time; the selection of tasty stuff lasts for several hours, until early afternoon, although the busiest time is probably between ten and eleven. This is a major *okazuya*, whose specialties include baked *char siu manapua*, and they sell an awful lot of pork hash. The chicken *chow fun* is mostly rice noodle and not much chicken, but vegetable half moons, stuffed with shrimp, vegetables, or pork, go out by the dozen and so do baked curry half moons. Roast chickens glisten behind the glass, and sweet-and-sour spareribs come in a heavy, luscious sauce. It's pretty much been that way since the Chin family started the business twenty-seven years ago. Nothing much has changed over the years (except the prices), especially not the red and white sign out front whose letters advertise the peanut candy they make—overflowing with peanuts and sesame seeds. Plus, they make their own cookies.

Bottom Line: Good, flavorsome takeout selection of Hawai'i's fast food.

SEKIYA'S RESTAURANT & DELICATESSEN

2746 Kaimukī Ave. • 732-1656
Tuesday–Thursday 8:30 a.m.-10 p.m.
Friday–Saturday 8:30 a.m.-11 p.m., Sunday 8:30 a.m.-9:45 p.m.
BYOB? Yes • Credit cards? Yes
$4-$12

It'd be difficult to find another combination quite like this in the islands: *okazuya*, sit-down Japanese restaurant—and soda fountain service (although no actual fountain), all in one. But the neighborhood obviously loves it, and since 1956 it's often been waiting-room only, with the owners' family members dishing out much the same food since the original *okazuya* was founded downtown in 1935. Be aware that certain delicatessen items, like fish patty, fried noodles, lima beans, and a handful of others, are sold only up at the counter—but then you're free to find a table. The high-ceilinged room, seating about sixty, is nothing exciting, with featureless vinyl booths and tables. It's the food. They use the same broth for all of the noodle dishes, which are extremely popular, from hot or cold *somen* to udon and *saimin*, the broth of squid and shrimp and chicken bones bubbling away all day in big pans on the stoves in back. Nearly everyone who eats here also orders a large *inari* sushi, certainly one of the best in town. The vegetable tempura batter is thick and puffy, but the batter on the shrimp tempura comes out exceptionally crisp. Breakfast eaters order mostly *saimin*—but dinner is where the full-course meals really kick in: sukiyaki, *donburi*, teriyaki steak, cutlets, and omelets.

Bottom Line: There's a whole lot of slurpin' goin' on at this long-lasting, hugely popular neighborhood institution.

IZAKAYA NONBEI

3108 'Olu St. • 734-5573
daily 5 p.m.-12 p.m.
BYOB? No, beer and wine served • Credit cards? Yes
per person: $10-$22

The first time I was in Izakaya Nonbei I was sitting at the bar, thinking I was just about finished eating but debating whether to order another Sapporo beer before heading home. "You know," said the waitress in passing, "we do our own pot stickers, and they're really good." She'd obviously noticed that I'd been experimenting with the menu, so I couldn't resist trying her *gyoza*. She was right. Dipped into a tangy chili sauce, those little darlings were a perfect ending. Since then, there have been other fine endings at this Japanese pub decorated with sake bottles and Japanese artifacts in an obscure location just off Kapahulu Boulevard. The sake feeling flows through the room, with Japanese music in the background, and there's always a feeling of warmth and neighborhood, plus good service. I'd begin with *karei karaage*—crisp, deep-fried flounder that comes with a dipping sauce to which you'd add spicy daikon. Eat the whole dish: head, bones, and all—they're the best part. Then a small dish of *nasu no kinoko itame,* that gentle helping of inoki mushrooms and Japanese eggplant sautéed in sake. Depending on the time of year, there might also be mushroom soup with seafood, served in a small, teapot-like vessel and poured into tiny sipping cups. Careful, they can be real hot to the touch. The sashimi is as fresh as it gets, and yes, that first night I did have another bottle of Sapporo—just to wash down the *gyoza*.

Bottom Line: If it's good enough for a regular like Hawai'i's famed Chef Mavro, it's good enough for the rest of us.

LEONARD'S BAKERY

933 Kapahulu Ave. • 737-5591
daily 6 a.m.-9 p.m.
BYOB? No • Credit cards? Yes
per person: $1.50-$3.00

The Portuguese were the ones who brought the pastry—Hawaiʻi's enormously popular malassada—with them when they came to the islands, but it's turned out that this fried doughnut-without-a-hole has come off better in Hawaiʻi than it does back on the Iberian Peninsula. If you don't believe me, try it in Portugal, then hie yourself into Leonard's and try one. Today, it's Lenny Rego, son of the original Leonard who began turning out his pastries in 1952, who's running the show, but the product is still just delicious; it melts in your mouth. Certainly as good as in the old days, when Leonard senior was vending at local fairs, a precursor to the Leonard's trucks you sometimes see dishing out hot malassadas in shopping center parking lots today. Yep, they've got a reputation, but rightly so. There may be lots of other bakery items in those display cases in the original, undistinguished building on the corner of Kapahulu and Charles Street, but how often do you need a decorated cake (although actually, they're pretty tasty themselves)? They're turning the malassadas out all the time, keeping the frying oil clean, so they're always warm, always yeasty and soft, just fabulous. Try them without the dusting of granulated sugar if you don't want to get your hands grainy while you're sitting out in front on the bench that's the only seating Leonard's provides. Still, do take out plenty of napkins.

Bottom Line: Eat 'em right away; malassadas don't go well unless they're hot, or at least warm, and these may be the best.

Mr. Ojisan

★
Da Bes'

1018 Kapahulu Ave. • 735-4455
Monday–Friday 11 a.m.-2 p.m., Monday–Thursday 5:30 p.m.-11 p.m.
Friday–Saturday 5:30 p.m.-1 a.m.
BYOB? No, full bar. • Credit cards? Yes
per person: $7-$18

Some refer to the small restaurant as a Japanese tavern, but it seems to me it's more like a bistro, a very good contemporary bistro. With its tiny selection of hard liquors on the back bar, if they're really pressed the staff might even put together a martini. But who really wants that when you can join the locals in enjoying a fine selection of sakes, or a bottle of cold Japanese beer? The room seats perhaps two dozen, with just three seats at the black-surfaced bar and several tables boasting the implements for preparing sukiyaki and *yosenabe*. "Japanese cuisine with a local flair," is what the slogan is here, but it turns out that the "local flair" is more in the fresh island ingredients and, says Keiko, a waitress who's been there since an earlier location in Waikīkī before they moved to Kapahulu in 1998, "the employees." She's right, the employees are great, almost as good as the food. Favorite appetizers include a scrumptious casserole of chives with egg, sizzling in the pan; or fried tofu with ginger, green onions. and grated turnips. For main dishes you'll go far before finding a better *ramen*, with its rich broth in which the meats, vegetables, and noodles blend deliciously, a meal in itself. Another favorite is *wafu* steak, a small ribeye flavored with *shoyu* and sake, garlic chips, onions, and grated turnip—a piece of meat that can be a bit chewy but comes bursting with flavor.

Bottom Line: Beautifully prepared Japanese dishes well served by a cordial staff.

Island of Oʻahu • Waikīkī to Hawaiʻi Kai • Kapahulu

37

ONO HAWAIIAN FOODS

726 Kapahulu Ave. • 737-2275
Monday–Saturday 11 a.m.-7:45 p.m.
BYOB? Yes • Credit cards? No
per person: $5-$10

"Be cool, no get mad." That's what the hand-lettered sign in front says, but heck, no one in the perpetual line at the front door of Hawaiʻi's best-known maker of *laulau, lomi* salmon, *kālua* pig and anything else in Hawaiian food would even think of getting mad. They're used to waiting for one of the thirty seats in the cramped room with its scuffed linoleum floor, the walls slathered with photos of celebrities as well as locals, run for forty-three years by the family of which ninety-year-old Sueko Oh Young is still the matriarch. If you're fortunate, you'll get to squeeze into a corner seat, where you can watch the food coming out and listen to the hubbub of conversation as people plunge into their favorite Hawaiian dishes. *Laulau* is a big deal: maybe the best in town, bursting with tender pork and lots of it. Peppery *pipikaula* is a dish for which patrons come miles, and if you're a devotee of *naʻau puaʻa*, this is the place to enjoy that pungent dish. Combination plates, featuring flavorsome *kālua* pig, rich chicken long rice and *lomi* salmon are the best way to sample a variety, but the à la carte selection considerably broadens the fun. On Mondays they serve chopped steak—perhaps not their strongest suit—but on Tuesdays they serve beef stew, the real thing. Every meal comes with the obligatory small dishes of onion and Hawaiian salt, plus a dash of *haupia*, and where else can you find a luscious dish like chicken watercress soup, the crisp greens scattered into a succulent home-made broth?

Bottom Line: Outstanding variety of dishes—some excellent—at Honolulu's best-known Hawaiian food restaurant, plus a choice of fresh or day-old poi.

RAINBOW DRIVE IN

3308 Kana'ina Ave. • 737-0177
daily 7:30 a.m.-9 p.m.
BYOB? No • Credit cards? No
per person: $2-$5

If, by good fortune, you happen to be a guest at Waikīkī's posh Halekūlani Hotel, and ask the concierge where to find good, really "local" food, you know where they send you? You've got it. You'll find yourself at the corner of Kana'ina and Kapahulu Avenues, where for over forty years the Ifuku family has been busy building what's become a plate lunch institution. We're not talking about much aesthetically: two order windows and formed concrete and plastic tables at an unappetizing covered outside eating area that's always busy. In the mornings and through the afternoons there's a constant stream of local labor force to the order windows, augmented by occasional hungry visitors from across town, and as the afternoon wears on citizens on their way home from the beach stop in to load up for dinner. Weekends, the busiest time, are jammed with beachgoers, the parking lot swarming with motorcycle clubs and bicyclists. Plate lunch is king, but some discretion is called for, even if everything is a tremendous value. Big reputation for the chili and beans on rice—a reputation well deserved, although all too often there's a hand-lettered sign saying, "no more chili." The macaroni salad, slightly peppery, is the best side dish, and even though popular plates like corned beef hash and BBQ teriyaki steak are worth the money, they're not worth a rave. What's worth a rave is the BBQ teriyaki pork sandwich, a ton of dripping meat in a soft bun, surrounded by lettuce and slathered with mayonnaise. Needs a pile of napkins. All this, and they've actually got parking too.

Bottom Line: Great prices, big helpings, easy in and out and plenty of good food.

SUNRISE RESTAURANT

525 Kapahulu Ave. • 737-4118
Monday–Saturday 11:30 a.m.-2 p.m., 5:30 p.m.-9 p.m.
BYOB? Yes • Credit cards? Yes
per person: $6-$15

Chokatsu and Kiyoko Tamayose have been running their little restaurant for five years now, but the feeling you get—the repeat customers, the cordiality, the simplicity of the space—is that you've walked into a neighborhood spot in a middle-sized Japanese town and that it's been there forever. It's hard to find, tucked around the corner off Kapahulu Avenue on Herbert Street next to Waiola Shave Ice. Inside, the small sushi bar hosts six wooden chairs, and the rest of the room is tables for a couple of dozen other diners, many of whom seem to know one another. At lunch, customers read newspapers, watch a game on the television in the corner, or discuss which fish in the case looks best. And it is mostly fish, although on the menu there's a certain Okinawan influence in dishes like pork tofu or stir-fried vegetables. Otherwise, it's baked oysters, butterfish, maybe a crispy *ika geso*. Often, Kiyoko will recommend *hamachi kama*, a meatier version than you'll find in many restaurants, and their dynamite is done with whatever seafood is freshest that day. Occasionally in the evenings Chokatsu, when he's not in the kitchen or cutting sushi, comes out, grabs a stringed instrument, and treats his guests to Okinawan folk songs. And if fish or folksongs are not for everyone, you'll go far before finding a better oxtail soup, with its pure broth, plenty of meat, and a certain appealing clarity in the flavor. Don't forget to mix in the fresh ginger that comes on the side.

Bottom Line: It's small, and the clientele loves the simplicity and the food, so you just might need reservations.

TOKKURI TEI

611 Kapahulu Ave. • 739-2800
Monday–Friday 11 a.m.-2 p.m.
Monday–Saturday 5:30 p.m.-12:00 midnight
BYOB? No • Credit cards? Yes
per person: $18-$26

Since 1989 Kazuhiro Mitake's cozy Tokkuri Tei in Kapahulu has been one of the most welcoming Japanese restaurants in town, dishing out a variety of appetizing dishes from an exceptionally adventurous menu. Much of the clientele is neighborhood, but you're just as likely to be talking to a "foodie" next to you at the sushi bar who's come from across town to try a new sake or a sushi roll. Stuck into a mini-mall behind a Papa John's Pizza, the room is flavored with colored paper lanterns, the walls covered with shelves of proprietary sake bottles and posters. "Is it always this busy?' you ask a fellow customer on a Tuesday night. "Hey," is the answer, "this isn't bad at all," and still there are people waiting to crowd into the place. Besides a chart describing and grading the sake selection, the menu also features hard spirits, and at the sushi bar you'll go far before finding a better dynamite roll, crammed with baked king clam, scallops, and onion, laced with hot sauce, green onions, and tempura flakes. From the grill comes scrumptious peeled eggplant in a sweet house sauce. Not too hungry? Try a grilled ear of sweet Kahuku corn. Or a salad of crisp salmon skins over tofu, or mini pork *katsu,* or enoki mushrooms sautéed with butter and seasoned with *shoyu.* Tasty tidbits include skewers of grilled beef tongue, squid legs, fresh tofu, *shiso,* and pork. Soups and pot dishes, sashimi plates, and *shabu shabu* also grace the bill of fare.

Bottom Line: The smiling waitress who leans over your shoulder to fill your cup from a big sake bottle also delivers some of the islands' most succulent Japanese dishes.

EGGS 'N THINGS

1911B Kalākaua Ave. • 949-0820
Monday–Wednesday 6 a.m.-2 p.m.
Thursday–Sunday 11 p.m.-2 p.m.
BYOB? No • Credit cards? No
per person: $6-$8

Back in 2002 you'd see people walk up to the storefront window, try to peer inside, and walk disappointedly away. After all, in its location on the ground floor of a high-rise building on the Honolulu edge of Waikīkī, Eggs 'n Things had been a breakfast fixture since 1974. Regular Waikīkī tourists would walk over from the hotels (parking is impossible) every time they hit town, and lots of locals agreed it was about the best breakfast place in the area. So lots of diners, especially those who like their eggs, pancakes, and sausages in either the early or very late hours, were pleased when Janice Fukunaga reopened after a severe fire, and today the place is going strong again. There's been some redecorating, but the large, bright room, small blond tables, and smiling waitresses—some who've been there over twenty years—in long, flowery split-leg aprons are still serving pretty much the same menu. To start with, there's a good selection of fresh island juices, including pineapple, mango, papaya, and banana. Then there are specials, like smoked pork chop and eggs, with the usual side selections of rice, pancakes, or potatoes. The pancakes are great, light and fluffy with an interesting selection of syrups from which to choose, like coconut, orange, or guava. Omelets can be just so-so, without too much character, but you have to say they're not stingy on the fillings.

Bottom Line: You're looking at a well-prepared American-style breakfast with some special Hawaiian touches.

PHÔ TRI

478 'Ena Rd. • 944-1190
daily 10 a.m.-10 p.m.
BYOB? Yes • Credit cards? Yes
per person: $5-$11

This is not your Chinatown *phô* joint, surrounded by a dozen similar Vietnamese restaurants. For one thing, the seasonings in their dishes are a little less invigorating than you might find downtown, and for another, the room of red Naugahyde booths and gray tiled floors is attractive and quiet, perhaps because, after all, it's in Waikīkī, even if hidden behind a 7-11 market just off Kalākaua. This is an easy place in which to actually dine on *phô* and a few other dishes, rather than just run in and slurp soup. George Nguyen, who learned his trade at his brother's restaurant in town before he opened his own six years ago, has, in fact, already opened a second branch not far away. When you ladle the first hot spoonful of Nguyen's *phô* into your mouth, you get that feeling of contentment and comfort that good soup often brings. Add fresh greens and sprouts, a dash or two of hot chile sauce, fish sauce, or hoisin, and you won't have to go to Chinatown, or even up to Kapi'olani Boulevard or King Street, for a *phô* fix. Nguyen's broth also distinguishes itself with especially good meats, a choice that includes eye-of-round steak, tendon, brisket, flank, tripe, and meatballs. Plus, he's successfully avoided the pitfall of so many other *phô* restaurants—where the soup may be very good but nothing else on the menu is—in dishes such as softly cooked lemon chicken or barbecued pork sirloin slices. They do leave on the television set that's at one end of the room, but the volume is turned way down.

Bottom Line: They go easy on the seasonings but put out a fine broth with good meats at this quiet, comfortable establishment.

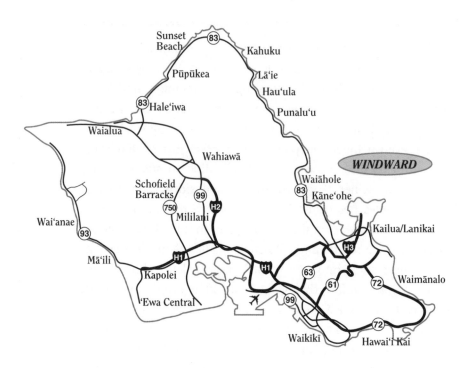

WINDWARD

Kailua
Agnes' Portuguese Bake Shop
Boots & Kimo's Homestyle Kitchen
Kailua Bar-B-Q
Pinky's Pupu Bar & Grill
Willow Tree

Kāneʻohe
Chao Phya Thai Restaurant
Junie's Coffee Shop
Kin Wah Chop Suey
Koa Pancake House
Masa & Joyce

Lanikai
Buzz's Original Steak House

Waiāhole
Ono Loa Hawaiian Foods

Waimānalo
Keneke's
Olomana Golf Links Restaurant

AGNES' PORTUGUESE BAKE SHOP

40 Hoʻolai St. • 262-5367
Tuesday–Sunday 6 a.m.-6 p.m.
BYOB? No • Credit cards? Yes
per person: $3-$8

Agnes herself has been retired to that Bake Shop in the Sky for a while, but for nearly thirty years her shop, now just a block off Kailua Road in the middle of Kailua, has been the sweetest place around. The open room in a gray building on the corner under a big bright yellow sign floods with light that bounces off glass-covered tables adorned with small vases of fresh flowers and pink tablecloths. The pastries that go with this tea shop–like environment are probably the best on the Windward side; in fact they're sold to restaurants all over the island. The display cases are filled with flaky Danish pastries, bulging jelly doughnuts, giant cinnamon rolls, chocolate crunch bars, pies, and breads. Especially breads: potato breads, multigrain breads, and Portuguese sweet breads. Most of Agnes' goodies are sold to go: pies by the dozen and warm loaves of bread and malassadas—doughier than most and with a hole in the middle. A tiny list of hot dishes includes Portuguese bean soup crammed with carrots, potatoes, ham shank, Portuguese sausage, onions, cabbage, tomatoes, celery, and beans (fortunately for the soup there's Tabasco sauce on the tables), and there's usually another soup or two, such as minestrone or miso. To go with that is a long list of Italian cream sodas, plus an equally long list of boutique coffees. Among the yummiest desserts: moist bread pudding made with sweet bread, rich with raisins and cinnamon and apple and coconut. Or try the chocolate brownie, heavy and rich and nutty.

Bottom Line: Luscious desserts, with a handful of soups providing an excuse to drop in for a meal.

BOOTS & KIMO'S HOMESTYLE KITCHEN

★
Da Bes'

131 Hekili St. • 263-7929
Tuesday–Friday 7 a.m.-2 p.m., Saturday–Sunday 6 a.m.-2 p.m.
BYOB? No • Credit cards? No
per person: $4-$9

The wall to the right as you walk in is decorated in sports memorabilia and boxes of Wheaties, "Breakfast of Champions." But fear not, nothing in the diner-like room of blues, blacks, and chrome tastes anything like Wheaties. Quite the contrary: nearly everything coming out of the kitchen at this Kailua standard, across the street from Pali Lanes, is to die for. Jess and Rick Kiakona own the place, but "Mom" is usually at the back by the cash register counting the receipts, even though she says, "I just work here," which is what she's been saying since the family began dishing out their *ʻono kau kau* in 1994. In restaurants, there are pancakes and there are pancakes; the dish for which Rick and Jess are best known—by locals as well as by tourists who've gotten the word and make their way through the tunnels to Windward Oʻahu—is banana pancakes with macadamia nut sauce. Now that's a dish! It's so laden with the sweet, distinctive sauce you can't even see the pancakes underneath, but they're there, chewy and fluffy at the same time, a fabulous treat. Hot sandwiches and omelets are a big part of the menu, but after the pancakes, next best is *pūlehu* ribs—shortribs cut thick and, in this case, seasoned only with Hawaiian salt, juicy and tender and covered with nearly blackened grilled Kula onions and mushrooms. More *ʻono.* Hamburger steak, also with grilled onions and mushrooms, is nearly as good. Now you see why, when you showed up outside, there were people on benches waiting for those three dozen seats.

Bottom Line: Lots of laughter, Hawaiian-friendly service, and good food.

KAILUA BAR-B-Q

590 Kailua Rd. • 262-5122
Monday–Saturday 8 a.m.-5:30 p.m., Sunday 8 a.m.-4 p.m.
BYOB? No • Credit cards? No
per person: $4-$7

In the afternoons after school Boram Hong is likely to be sitting in a corner behind the serving counter, hunched over a book and waiting to help. Boram says it's a textbook, but for all we know it's Danielle Steele. Anyhow, she's Sua Torii's teenage daughter, and Sua owns this small eatery sandwiched (pun intended) between a Times supermarket and a bookstore in downtown Kailua. Some very succulent dishes come across that serving counter, and Boram jumps up and helps when needed, but it's more often Sua who's up front serving. She bought the business, which has been there for eight years, only two years ago. It's not much more than a storefront, with five plastic chairs, a couple of tiny eating counters, and several outdoor tables nearby. The feeling inside is of fresh cooking, even late in the day, and the plates of food bear that out. If the fried *man doo* are too hot to eat immediately, the crusts just a little crispy, why, pick up a cheap used paperback (is this the place for Danielle Steele?) from the rack outside the bookstore while they cool down. *Limu* combines crunch and chewiness in its mix of cucumber and onion, and the meat *jun* is one of the best on the Windward side, eggy and almost creamy, and barbecue chicken is another tempting choice. Other dishes worth ordering in these— need we say?—large portions, are *mochiko* chicken and chicken long rice.

Bottom Line: Better-than-average Korean barbecue with several especially tasty dishes.

48

PINKY'S PUPU BAR & GRILL

970 N. Kalāheo Ave. • 254-6255
Monday–Saturday 4 p.m.-10 p.m., Sunday 9 a.m.-10 p.m.
BYOB? No, full bar • Credit cards? Yes
per person: $7-$23

Big, light, casual, and full of light, with perhaps three hundred seats, the walls layered in Hawaiian kitsch, stuff you might see in the souvenir shops—that's Pinky's. When we say "locals" here—and there are a lot of them, in addition to Around-the-Island Tourists—we're talking families from the nearby Kailua suburbs plus "tons of Marines," as one of the bartenders says. Pinky's is right at the neck of the Mokapu Peninsula going out to the Kāne'ohe Marine Corps Air Station; and need we say we're talking "really jumping" weekends? They do a big bar business, pouring a lot of beer from draft choices like Samuel Adams, Newcastle, Budweiser, and Coors Light, and behind the bar is a good selection of bottled imports and boutique brews. One caveat: the drinks are a small pour—but the price is small too. Probably it's the pupus menu that's the best thing to order, with substantial portions of selections like *kālua* pig quesadilla—filled with pork, black beans, corn and cream—large *'ahi* cakes pan-fried with Asian coleslaw, or coconut crunchy calamari with a thick dipping sauce; lots of regular customers do a whole meal on pupus. Red meat is big on the entrée side, with prime rib served in several sizes. The quality of the prime ribs and the steaks are better, and the servings larger, than you'd expect from the menu pricing.

Bottom Line: Good food at decent prices tumbled together with lots of people and plenty of noise.

ISLAND OF O'AHU • WINDWARD • KAILUA

WILLOW TREE

25 Kāneʻohe Bay Drive • 254-1139
Monday–Saturday 11 a.m.-9:30 p.m.
BYOB? Yes • Credit cards? Yes
per person: $7-$10

The plate lunches served from the kitchen until four in the afternoon may be the spiffiest Korean plates on the island. Still, when the menu changes its format just a bit for dinner, and certain meat dishes come served on sizzling platters, things move up just a notch. Imagine a plate lunch place where you can actually "dine." That's because Willow Tree, in the Safeway shopping center by the back gate to the Kāneʻohe Marine base, really is a full restaurant and not just a plate lunch counter. The Yoo family, plus married-in member Alan Kirby, have been all over the place for fourteen years now—at the front door, in the kitchen, and serving tables. But maybe they ought to hide Kirby back in the kitchen, since—could this actually happen in Hawaiʻi?—he recommends assorted vegetables instead of macaroni salad as a side dish. Nearly everything begins with a bowl of turnip soup, with rice and kim chee on the side. Super dishes include fried spicy chicken wings in a special house *shoyu* sauce, and spicy barbecued pork. Yummy. The *juhn* dishes, meat or mahimahi, are pretty eggy and perhaps forgettable, but long rice or fried *man doo* are well worth ordering. They put out a mean shrimp tempura, and the ever-present *kal bi* is an appetizing plate. On request, meals end with roasted barley tea, sometimes sipped while chatting with Korean Navy sailors at the next table, on the island for joint military exercises.

Bottom Line: Good Korean dining, much of it barbecue style, in a family-run setting.

CHAO PHYA THAI RESTAURANT

45-480 Kāne'ohe Bay Dr. • 235-3555
daily 11 a.m.-2 p.m., 5 p.m.-9 p.m.
BYOB? Yes • Credit cards? Yes
per person: $8-$13

Sometimes it's the small things that count, beginnings and endings. Like a starting dish of crispy chicken wing appetizers stuffed with long rice, vegetables, ground chicken, and deep-fried ti, the steaming aroma of garlic enveloping the table. Or a dessert of coconut ice cream made in the back: one of the richest, creamiest and most delicious on the island. For sixteen years Angoon Coppedge, known in and around her restaurant in the Windward City Shopping Center as Mama Toy, has been on the floor greeting her mostly suburban clientele in a community that doesn't boast a lot of Thai restaurants. She's got a fairly conventional menu, but the locals know that, and so it's not a bad idea, if you're new, to lean over (or is that rude?) to see what the next table's having; a little Kāne'ohe input on just how hot you want your spicing in the green chicken curry—with eggplant and sweet basil, one of the better items—doesn't hurt. The classic *phad thai*, which Mama Toy calls newspaper noodles, is pretty appealing, as is the popular Chao Phya salad, with lettuce, cucumbers, tomatoes, onions, and tofu cubes, laced with chicken and shrimp in a sweet-and-sour coconut dressing. Perhaps a touch of caution is advised on the fish dishes; the basil mahimahi and the ginger fish, for instance, are lathered in lovely sauces, but occasionally there's a heavy hand in the kitchen and then they can arrive overcooked. The room itself? Bright, flowery murals on the walls, linens and china on the tables, and a white lattice ceiling.

Bottom Line: If you order right, you'll do okay here; the coconut ice cream itself is worth a drive.

JUNIE'S COFFEE SHOP

46-022 Kamehameha Hwy. • 247-1607
daily 6:30 a.m.-1 p.m. (closes earlier on weekends)
BYOB? No • Credit cards? No
per person: $6-$9

What can I say about Junie's except that it's a real "joint" in the best sense of the word—and it's got some of the best corned beef hash I've ever eaten. And talk about family! Suzanne Iwamoto is the proprietor, and she's usually there, as is her daughter Trisha, behind the counter. It was Trisha's grandmother (Junie) who started the place nearly forty years ago. Stuck in the rear corner of a small strip mall next door to the Kāneʻohe post office, the restaurant, I'm told, hasn't changed much since it opened. The couple of dozen seats—five of them at the counter—are a mixture of various chairs, and the ceiling fan and battered Formica counter make up the rest of the decor. The aroma of the good stuff coming off the grill meets you as you come through the door, perhaps because there's a lot of garlic on the menu. Although the wall menu boasts *saimin* and hamburgers and teriyaki and a handful of other items, the really best things include the fresh banana hotcakes (no garlic in these, thank you), the heavy plate of fried pork chops smothered in gravy and onions, and the hash. That crispy, homemade dish comes with or without garlic, and it's worth the trip itself. No macaroni or potato salad here, but a small, refreshing bowl of fresh tomatoes and cucumbers.

Bottom Line: The best hash, in a real down-home Kāneʻohe joint.

KIN WAH CHOP SUEY

Da Bes'

45-588 Kamehameha Hwy. • 247-4812
daily 10 a.m.-9 p.m.
BYOB? No • Credit cards? Yes
per person: $7-$14

They've never let the name fool them, those hundreds of Kāne'ohe's knowledgeable Chinese food fans who think the Cantonese menu at Kin Wah is the most appetizing on the Windward side of the island. This is no chop suey joint; of perhaps 150 dishes on the menu, only four are chop suey, and more than a handful of the restaurant's devotees swear it's the specials that bring the best out of the restaurant's kitchen. For over twenty years, regulars—and there are lots of them—have been pushing their way through the crowded parking lot back behind the Island MiniMart store on the highway to a rear building that houses the restaurant operated over the years by one or another branch of the Cheng family. Most of the enthusiasts aren't coming for chop suey; they're there for those specials, for dishes such as yummy Singapore noodles: a heaping curried platter of *mai fun* noodles mixed with shards of shrimp, vegetables, pork, and egg. Or wonderfully flavorsome pot roast spareribs: tender, boneless, meaty chunks served in a sweet-and-sour gravy. Or menu dishes like crispy chicken *gau gee mein:* pork hash–filled fried won ton on a platter crammed with succulent noodles, chicken, and perfectly stir-fried vegetables. And down in a corner of the menu are the popular sizzling platters, highlighted by the combination seafood with vegetables—they really do know how to do vegetables in this place. The restaurant is enhanced by offering a full bar menu in its two rooms of dark vinyl booths, white linen tablecloths, and large round family tables. Lunch can be busy, but dinner is even busier.

Bottom Line: Outstanding Cantonese specials, and you won't go wrong with the rest of the menu, either.

KOA PANCAKE HOUSE

46-126 Kahuhipa St. • 235-5772
daily 6:30 a.m.-2 p.m.
BYOB? No • Credit cards? Yes
per person: $4-$6

Oddly enough, pancakes aren't the best thing to order at this popular breakfast and lunch spot just off Kamehameha Highway in the industrial area of downtown Kāneʻohe. On weekends there can be twenty to thirty people milling around outside waiting for a table, and inside the lighting is surprisingly low for a breakfast place, vinyl booths nestling into wood trim. It's noisy and bustling, with fast, cordial waitresses who've got their own suggestions if pancakes are not for you. That Hawaiian staple, Portuguese sausage and eggs, is a good bet here, but owners Jai W. and Kyung Sung, who took over from his sister a couple of years ago (there's another Koa over in Wahiawā, but it's takeout only), haven't been afraid to give the neighbors an eclectic bill of fare. Where else can you order *mahi* benedict, an uncommon dish with a tangy benedict sauce that soaks into the English muffin with the fish and gets rich and gooey? And we don't often find a menu that offers *vinha d'alhos* omelet, crammed with pork marinated in vinegar, garlic, and chile oil. Or something as simple as a mouth-watering omelet of sour cream and chives. Most popular dishes at lunchtime are the chicken teriyaki, seafood combo, and *kal bi* beef.

Bottom Line: A solid place to go for breakfast, with a couple of good dishes you won't find often.

MASA & JOYCE

45-582 Kamehameha Hwy. • 235-6129
Monday 9 a.m.-6 p.m., Wednesday–Friday 9 a.m.-6 p.m.
Saturday 9 a.m.-4 p.m., Sunday 9 a.m.-2 p.m.
BYOB? Yes • Credit cards? Yes
per person: $4-$8

The small fish market Masa and Joyce Tobaru opened twenty-five years ago in the Koʻolau Center across the street from Temple Valley ended up with the tail wagging the dog. The original's still there, but today the main store, where all the action is, is in Kāneʻohe across Kamehameha Highway from the Foodland market. The newer one—quite properly labeled an *okazuya*—is much larger, with plenty of room for half a dozen comfortable tables and bigger food display cases. The beckoning cases draw a constant flow of seafood fans, even though the menu has expanded well beyond that. Still, it's the huge slabs of obviously fresh *ʻahi* that first grab the eye as you walk in, some of it already cut into packaged sashimi, and next to that are trays of a rotating selection of *poke*, ranging from hot and sweet with onion to the more esoteric—like *kukui* nut with Hawaiian salt, *limu,* and green onion. In a couple of adjoining cases are a limited sushi selection, featuring California rolls and teri beef rolls. If you're a purist you may not like the mayonnaise in the rolls, but the *inari* sushi is worth taking home, with maybe a couple of *aku* sticks. To fill the plastic takeout boxes they're also making fish and corned beef hash patties, plus teriyaki chicken, grilled fish, rice balls, and shrimp and vegetable tempuras. If it happens that you're heading to the airport, this is a good place to stop in and pick up a bento: as you might imagine, it's the seafood *donburi* that's the best bet.

Bottom Line: Long-standing, reliable seafood *okazuya*.

Buzz's Original Steak House

413 Kawailoa Rd. • 261-4661
daily 11 a.m.-9 p.m.
BYOB? No, full bar. • Credit cards? No
per person: $18-$35

Buzz himself has been gone for years, the restaurant that still has his name on it in Waikīkī is no longer in the family, and yes, there is a newer Buzz operation in Pearl City. But the older, "authentic" Buzz's is still going strong by the stream across the street from Kailua Beach, owned by Buzz's ex-wife, Bobby Lou Yeackel. For over forty years now this steak and seafood house has remained a congenial, cozy restaurant, the varnished tropical woods in keeping with its role as a cross between an old Don the Beachcomber and a newer Chart House. The bar even puts out its share of those fancy tropical drinks, with Jack Daniel's and Stolichnaya vodka classily included in the "well" list. You can sit in the darkened inside, or outside on the enclosed patio, where the ambiance loses a bit because the patio is right on the edge of the road. The menu, written on handcarved wooden planks, includes a modest but better than ordinary salad bar with the entrées. Although lunch—which attracts its share of tourists from Waikīkī—is mostly hefty hamburgers and big salads, evening eats include a popular top sirloin (10 ounces), or an almost equally popular prime rib (although it's not, alas, served on the bone), with crispy, firm steak fries on the side and several fresh local fish offerings. The fish is darned good, prepared several different ways and always delicately cooked in whatever manner is appropriate to the particular fish. But perhaps, for those of us with more plebeian tastes, the best dish on the menu is the ground sirloin special, covered with sautéed mushrooms and onions. Melts in your mouth.

Bottom Line: Quality meat and fish at a price better than you'd expect.

ONO LOA HAWAIIAN FOODS

48-140 Kamehameha Hwy. • 239-2863
daily except Thursday and Sunday, 10:30 a.m.-2 p.m.
BYOB? Yes • Credit cards? No
per person: $6-$7

'Ono loa means "very delicious," an apt name for this roadside surprise in the historic Waiāhole Poi Factory shack on Kamehameha Highway at the mouth of Waiāhole Valley. It seems appropriate that Maxine Prudencio, who's been making classic Hawaiian dishes there for six years now, lives just up the valley and grows her own taro; that's undoubtedly why the poi is so good. And, fortunately for us, so is everything else. The location, nearly as rural as you can find and still be on O'ahu, means you've got to take it home or to the beach, although if you're really eager—so hungry you can't wait—there are two shaded picnic tables on one side of the building. Maxine's pork or chicken *laulau* are heavy with meat and taro leaves, and the *lomi* salmon isn't bad. Her chicken long rice is among the best and most flavorsome on the island, the *kālua* pig in the same rank. What I like best really isn't even Hawaiian: she puts out a wonderful tripe stew, flavorfully loaded with carrots, celery, tripe, and potatoes. And then there are the pork and banana *pasteles*—the meat tender, the enveloping mashed banana moist and flavorful. The silky *haupia* is worth the trip out to the north shore of Kāne'ohe itself, especially if you order chocolate. And how often do we find that taro root–based sweet called *kūlolo?* Chewy and sweet, it's a unique, hard-to-find dessert. "I make the food," says Maxine, "the way I like it."

Bottom Line: Fine Hawaiian food in a rural roadside shack, with some interesting dishes you won't easily find elsewhere.

KENEKE'S

41-857 Kalaniana'ole Hwy. • 259-9800
daily 9:15 a.m.-5:15 p.m.
BYOB? Yes • Credit cards? No
per person: $3-$6

ISLAND OF O'AHU • WINDWARD • WAIMĀNALO

The bald, bearded guy who's usually behind the serving window is Hawaiian-big, but it's all muscle. Keith Ward just happens to hold a bunch of powerlifting titles, and while you're waiting for a plate you can read his biography in newspaper articles on the walls. He's had the faded lunch place on the highway near Waimānalo Beach Park since 1984, and if the aging white, blue, and red building wasn't an institution before that, it's certainly become one now. Sunburned beach visitors mix in the hot sun out front with locals waiting for their orders, and at the next window there's often a line waiting for the refreshing, flaky shave ice. It's a real island highway feeling here, a casual side-of-the-road atmosphere that's kept tranquilized by the surprising softness of the proprietor's voice as he calls out your order. Seating is at tables inside— where the walls are plastered with biblical quotations—as well as outdoors. *Laulau* is a popular item on the menu, but they don't make their own, and I'd order something else instead. Like pork *guisantes,* which they serve as a lovely, savory plate, or a deluxe teri burger, slightly crisped, or perhaps a mildly spicy *kālua* pig plate. If you're in a breakfast mood, there's a Spam, egg, and cheese sandwich that's okay, and they do a good job on steak fries.

Bottom line: A fun roadside spot for beachgoers, locals, and 'round-the-island drivers in a plate lunch mood.

OLOMANA GOLF LINKS RESTAURANT

41-1801 Kalaniana'ole Hwy. • 259-5163
6 a.m.-6 p.m. (variable, depending on golf activities)
BYOB? No, full bar • Credit cards? Yes
per person: $5-$9

There's an extensive list of pupus, most customers wear golf caps and shorts, and the bar keeps busy drawing cold pitchers of draft beer. What else would you expect in a restaurant to the public, that also doubles as the social side of the clubhouse for a private golf course? The restaurant, set off the highway on the Kailua end of town, also happens to be the only real sit-down eating in Waimānalo. Both restaurant and golf course were opened in 1967, and the dining room probably hasn't changed much since then. The decor is rattan and patterned island fabrics, making the large room a nice place to sit in the afternoons to enjoy the view out the large plate glass windows over the course and up to the south end of the Ko'olau mountain range. In the morning the three-egg, fried rice omelet, topped with slabs of fried luncheon meat, is what golfers seem to prefer before hitting the links, but a better-than-average corned beef hash is pretty popular too. Personally, I go for the banana pancakes, which come slightly crisped. The most popular pupus, which they begin serving at midmorning, are crispy, heavily breaded chicken wing flings, fried *saimin* noodles, or *kālua* pork mixed with cabbage—a very good dish indeed. Sandwiches could best be described as uninspired, but the hamburger steak, smothered in gravy and onions, is a flavorful selection from the hot entrée list.

Bottom Line: The only game in town if you want to sit down and dine from a decent menu in Waimānalo.

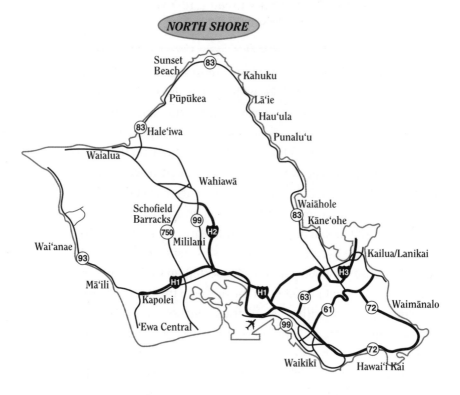

NORTH SHORE

Hale'iwa
Hale Wai Drive In
Kua Aina Sandwich Shop

Kahuku
Amy's by the Greene
Giovanni's Original White Shrimp Truck
Kahuku Famous Shrimp
Lei Lei's Bar & Grill

Lā'ie
Hukilau Café

Punalu'u
Punaluu Restaurant

Pūpūkea
Sharks Cove Grill

Sunset Beach
Taste of Paradise Surf Grill
Ted's Bakery

Waialua
Waialua Fast Foods & Catering

HALE WAI DRIVE IN

66-412 Hale'iwa Rd. • 637-6054
daily 7 a.m.-8 p.m.
BYOB? No • Credit cards? No
per person: $3-$6

Hawai'i's biggest reputation in a hamburger, Kua Aina, is only minutes away. But this little spot, hidden away on a back road near the ocean in a Hale'iwa residential neighborhood, dishes out its own little jewel. Theirs is a small, peppery, homemade hamburger patty, crisp on the outside and served on a soft bun, lathered with mayonnaise and ketchup and packed with lettuce, onion, and tomato. It gives the big guys a run for their money. The setting is pretty simple: four tables in an open, roofed seating area adjoining the order window in a faded green concrete block building shared with Chun's Market. The plate lunches, hamburger, and daily specials have been drawing nearby farm workers, laborers, and surfers off the main highway for over thirty years. Much of the business is takeout, a lot of it in the form of the hefty plate lunches. They've got the proverbial macaroni salad, of course, and scoops of rice, plus a centerpiece dish like grilled mahimahi, or tender spareribs in a slightly sweet gravy, or big chunks of beef cooked to tenderness and served with a curry sauce; or the *saimin*, crammed with vegetables and noodles.

Bottom Line: A simple joint with good food at a good price.

Kua Aina Sandwich Shop

66-160 Kamehameha Hwy. • 637-6067
daily 11 a.m.-8 p.m.
BYOB? No • Credit cards? No
per person: $8-$10

For nearly thirty years the luscious aroma of grilling meat has hovered over Hale'iwa's main street as patrons come from far and wide for a mouthful of Hawai'i's most famous hamburger (locations also in Japan, Honolulu, and California). In early 2004 the shop moved to a larger location a few doors from the original, taking with it the dramatic surfing photographs on the walls, as well as a reputation. You're still lucky if you can find a table inside or outside, but outside is a good spot from which to watch the long white stretch limousines pull up and disgorge their hamburger-seeking foreign travelers. Okay, the reputation is there, but the hamburger itself? It just no longer seems as good—if ever it was—as its reputation, and these days at least a couple of other items on the menu are, simply, better. Kua Aina may have the best French fries on the island, skinny almost to the point of being shoestrings, homemade and cooked to a crisp with the skins on. The bacon, lettuce, and tomato sandwich on toast is outstanding, with crisp, thick bacon and plenty of mayonnaise. The mahimahi sandwich is also a winner, cooked perfectly. Although you get a choice of sandwich rolls, usually the specialty of the house (either a third or a half pound of meat, a commercial patty that frequently comes overcooked) is served on a Kaiser, in this case a completely undistinguished bun. We do concede that the fixings—lots of lettuce, tomato, grilled onions, and mayonnaise—are perfect.

Bottom Line: Hawai'i's Big Reputation hamburger place has better menu choices than its specialty.

AMY'S BY THE GREENE

56-485 Kamehameha Hwy. • 293-8896
Monday–Saturday 7 a.m.-3 p.m.
BYOB? Yes • Credit cards? No
per person: $3-$5

"We learned to cook," is the way Diana Huddy starts out when she's asked how she got into the business. She had to: she was one of twelve kids. These days she's doing her cooking in a green concrete block and metal-roofed shack at the signal corner in Kahuku. Diana's right across the street from the school—and she's the first to admit that if you want to enjoy breakfast or lunch at one of her two long, covered picnic tables, don't do it before eight in the morning—when the kids are hanging out before school for a cigarette and maybe a plate of fried rice or a bacon and egg sandwich—or just after two, when school gets out. The rest of the day, she's dishing out breakfast plates described in golfing terms—she's just a couple of blocks from the local municipal course. Breakfast and plate lunches are the best of Diane's menu. Under Par is a hearty portion of eggs, fried rice, and lots of crisp *lup cheong.* That rice is up there with the best, moist but not gummy and filled with scallions, egg, pork, and fish cake. On the plate lunch list (they come in both full and minisizes), the favorites are hamburger steak and onions lathered with a heavy gravy, or deep-fried teri chicken, kept tender inside its crunchy skin. Naturally, since we're in the land of the shrimp truck, there's fried shrimp on the menu. All the plates go great with a beer, if you're smart enough to have gone across the street to the Kahuku Superette and picked up a bottle or two.

Bottom Line: Good breakfast plates and decent plate lunches in the middle of an old Oʻahu sugar town.

Giovanni's Original White Shrimp Truck

55-5050 Kamehameha Hwy. • 293-1839
daily 11 a.m.-6:30 p.m.
BYOB? Yes • Credit cards? No
per person: $11-$12

On an around-the-island jaunt it's hard to miss, there in the "middle" of Kahuku on the highway: an old white kitchen truck covered with signatures—my own included—usually surrounded by parked cars, motorcycles, and a white stretch limousine or two disgorging Japanese visitors. Reputedly this is *the* original highway shrimp truck in the islands, but whether it is or not, it comes complete with picnic tables under an awning, plumeria trees in the background, and large trash cans filled with remnants of shrimp plates. The tables are usually jammed with happy customers gobbling plates of spicy or garlicky shrimp and scrambling for their paper napkins in the breeze. The menu is a simple one: shrimp, although there is a small adjoining truck that sells fresh fruit smoothies. The most popular order is scampi: a half pound (10 to 12) of crustaceans marinated and then fried quickly in a ton of lovely crisp garlic and butter. If you want it hot and spicy you'll do well to notice the warning: "no refunds" on this baby. It's that hot, a great sauce made, they say, from Mozambique peppers and spices. If you go for it anyhow, the antidote is bringing in cold beer from the Kahuku Superette next door. The lemon-and-butter style is a perfectly insipid dish, the shrimp boiled to boredom and served with a dipping sauce. When a major national food magazine complimented Giovanni's recently they must have forgotten this dish. One tip: it's not on the menu, but if you ask, they've got a surprisingly good large, kosher-style hot dog, served with the scampi sauce on a delicious doughy bun.

Bottom Line: A fun spot on the highway with okay shrimp in a couple of delicious sauces.

KAHUKU FAMOUS SHRIMP

Kamehameha Hwy. • 455-1803
daily 10 a.m.-6 p.m.
BYOB? Yes • Credit cards? No
per person: $8-$11

Competition among Oʻahu's roadside shrimp truck entrepreneurs has revved up a notch in recent years. Claims to being the very first in Kahuku may be with Giovanni's Original, but three years ago, just two hundred yards up Kamehameha Highway in front of the old sugar mill, Jung Ku and wife Kyung Soon hung out their own shingle on a battered white kitchen truck, called it Kahuku Famous Shrimp, and began dishing out the goods. Some would consider this a spin-off, and perhaps that's so, but if the ten shrimp (about a half pound) on the plate are firm and succulent—maybe even better than the "original"—and the price is okay, then so what? The atmosphere is sticky purple picnic tables under a plastic awning, surrounded by hibiscus and plumeria. One thing is for sure: the menu at the newer arrival gives the diner a much greater choice. Although the garlic butter and hot and spicy versions of fried shrimp with rice and macaroni salad are the usual favorites, the shrimp and steak (eight-ounce New York) combination is a popular one, and so is the shrimp and veggie stir-fry. For my own money, the spicy squid is the best item on the bill of fare. If the kids don't like shrimp, let them try the coconut lemon shrimp, shelled and butterflied and so heavy with coconut they won't even taste the shellfish. A couple of pluses to this particular shrimp truck: you've got three choices in the strength of the hot sauce, and (I appreciate this) their shrimp is more thoroughly cracked and peeled back than some others, making it easier to eat. Ku and Soon own a saltwater shrimp farm in Wailua. With any luck, we'll soon be getting fresh instead of frozen.

Bottom Line: Good shrimp plus a handful of other tasty choices on the roadside of the North Windward shore.

Lei Lei's Bar & Grill

57-049 Kuilima Drive • 293-2662
daily 7 a.m.-11 a.m. (breakfast), 11 a.m.-10 p.m. (lunch, dinner)
BYOB? No, full bar • Credit cards? Yes
per person: $10-$25

Pickings are slim up on the North and North Windward Shores between Hale'iwa and Kāne'ohe, but for "dining"—and I don't mean chowing down on a plate lunch—Lei Lei's is it. When, in early 2002, new ownership began overhauling the Turtle Bay Resort, one of the things they did was bring in Ian Buscher and Mike Neubert as restaurateurs down at the golf course clubhouse. Between them the two had thirty years with Chart House, and even though we may not be talking Michelin stars, they're running a restaurant at Turtle Bay that's a big improvement on any Chart House I've ever seen. Sprawled inside and out in a contemporary Hawaiian motif, fronting a putting green and facing out over the course, the bar scene hosts the expected share of golfers, but although some of the clientele come down on the shuttle from the hotel, much of it is local. The bar—my own favorite place to eat—gives you a decent pour, and on some nights there's live Hawaiian music. Among the best appetizers are coconut-crunchy shrimp dipped in plum or cocktail sauce, or a large portion of 'ahi poke, always beautifully fresh. On the entrée side you can select either a full or half order of baby back ribs, roasted and grilled and served with a tangy barbecue sauce—the tender meat falling off the bone—or slow-roasted prime rib that comes in three sizes (including on the bone) with fabulous garlic smashed potatoes. A special, like macadamia-crusted mahimahi, is likely to melt in your mouth. It's not on the menu, but do try ordering an entrée "pupu style." And do you like oyster shooters?

Bottom Line: Best sit-down eating on this end of O'ahu, and fun besides.

HUKILAU CAFE

55-662 Wahinepeʻe St. • 293-8616
Tuesday–Friday 7 a.m.-2 p.m., Saturday 7 a.m.-11:30 a.m.
BYOB? No • Credit cards? No
per person: $4-$6

Let me be plain about this: the best down-home, local spot for breakfast on the North Windward shore is this obscure, little-bit-hard-to-find joint on a three-way corner a block off Hukilau Beach in Lāʻie. And their lunch isn't bad either. The story is that Hawaiʻi's renowned chef Sam Choy started here, that this was called Sam's Place years ago, but for the last ten years it's been run by Kalani Soren, who's usually busy behind the grill in the back. When it's full, the place holds maybe three dozen diners around assorted Formica tables—large people, mostly Hawaiians—most of whom know each other, with a smattering of staff and faculty from nearby Brigham Young University campus and an occasional tourist who's straggled in looking for "local color." There's always a lot of amiable conversation going on back and forth between tables. Foodwise, it's sometimes hard to choose. The Hawaiian sweet bread French toast is fabulous, rich and moist. But then there are the big plastic bowls filled with what they call beef stew omelet, the stew poured over a bed of rice and topped with a couple of eggs. Or the fried rice, filled with ham, green onions, and egg, perhaps with a side order of beautifully grilled Portuguese sausage. At lunch, the hands-down favorite is the roast pork plate lunch, although the Hukilau burger (hamburger, teri beef, grilled onion, cheese, and so on) is also an interesting selection.

Bottom Line: Good eating, big quantities, and fast, smiling service in a fun local spot.

Punaluu Restaurant

53-146 Kamehameha Highway • 237-8474
daily 11 a.m.-9 p.m.
BYOB? No, full bar. • Credit cards? Yes
per person: $7-$17

It's not the first incarnation of the low, tropical roadhouse nestled between Kamehameha Highway and the mountains under a shabby banyan tree. It was once the well-known Paniolo Cafe, and for a while it was Ahi's, and now maybe, just maybe, since Yong Chin took over three years ago, it's the real thing, "a place," Chin says, "to come and hang out, have a couple of drinks." It is comfortable, separated into several casual rooms, a welcoming wood-topped bar in the middle. In fact, it's the only bar in this rural piece of the North Windward coast—if you ignore the tour bus–supported Crouching Lion—and it's become the local hangout. The menu includes a handful of steaks, sandwiches, and salads, but seafood is what Chin, who is sometimes behind the bar, will recommend if you ask. Shrimp, especially shrimp—and this in a slice of the coast where there are probably ten roadside signs yelling "shrimp" within a fifteen-minute ride in each direction. Here, it comes tempura style, in cocktails, hot and spicy, and scampi style, but the most interesting has got to be in olive oil, garlic, and pineapple, a fascinating contrast in flavors. The shrimp combo's the best way to try 'em all. If not shrimp, then stuffed fish, usually either mahimahi or ono—Yong herself prefers the ono—stuffed with imitation crab and vegetables. Another good pick is the fish burger, thick with 'ahi, mahimahi, or ono and crunchy with a big slab of fresh onion and plenty of sauce. One lament: that's a pretty short pour at the bar.

Bottom Line: Decent food and good hanging out in an easy, jungly roadhouse with live music on the weekends.

SHARKS COVE GRILL

59-702 Kamehameha Hwy. • 638-8300
daily 11 a.m.-6 p.m.
BYOB? Yes • Credit cards? Yes
per person: $5-$8

We're talking Surferville here, but with a healthy twist, if not quite organic. Right across the highway from Sharks Cove and just down from the Foodland market, the small, attractive minipavilion sprang up off a newly poured concrete slab in mid-2003. The food's full of flavor, and owner Jacque Rarick's husband, Randy, is heavily involved in the local surfing community, so I'd look for this roadside eating to be around awhile. Although they've got their own version of a plate lunch—they've recently added pancakes, eggs, and taro toast as breakfast menu—it's not necessarily the usual two-scoop rice–macaroni salad model. The fresh fish sandwich is served on a large taro roll, lathered in a sauce and hugged by plenty of lettuce and tomato, both grown locally; best of all, the fish is lightly and tenderly cooked. Seating is outside under attractive white umbrellas surrounded by tropical plantings, with an occasional chicken or a wandering bird or two underfoot, and it's pretty comfortable to be able to look across the street to the rocks, the waves, and the ocean. If you're not in a fish sandwich mood, then there's the house specialty: skewers, like the appetizing pesto marinated shrimp, cooked just briefly and matched with bell peppers, mushrooms, zucchini, cherry tomatoes, and onions. Other skewers are fish, teriyaki chicken breast, or tri-tip. Plates come with rice, a small salad, and (here's a nice touch) Kahuku corn. Like things spicy? Try the Chinese chicken salad, with grilled chicken, fresh greens, and a sesame vinaigrette dressing—plus chunks of pineapple. Still looking for healthy living? Think veggie burger or Pūpūkea green salad.

Bottom Line: Nice spot to enjoy an easy lunch in the midst of the world's liveliest surf activity.

Taste of Paradise Surf Grill

59-254 Kamehameha Highway • 638-0855
daily 11:30 a.m.-9:30 p.m.
BYOB? Yes • Credit cards? No
per person: $6-$10

Out on the North Shore, where huge surf lures surfer and beachgoer alike, there's a big contingent of Brazilian surfers. When they came up from Ipanema, besides bringing bikinis and bossa nova with them, they brought food. Michele and Marcos Santos, straight out of Rio de Janeiro, set themselves up several years ago in what is best described as a plastic Quonset hut, a sort of light, airy greenhouse on the *mauka* side of Kamehameha Highway, tucked in behind the giant tiki in the heart of surfland between Waimea Bay and Sunset Beach. Their Taste of Paradise has turned out to be a light-end fish and salad place with some Brazilian touches—call it a Hawaiian highway diner without the heaviness. A handful of round tables is mixed with long blue picnic tables to which waitresses are busily carrying paper plates heavy with jumbo tiger shrimp marinated in lemon, garlic, and olive oil and grilled with pineapple, or fish fillets (frequently *'ahi*)—always fresh, but sometimes cooked with a slightly heavy hand—marinated in the chef's sauce and grilled. There's a handful of grilled sandwiches— fish, chicken, eggplant, and steak—with melted provolone—and a tasty Pipeline eggplant, smothered in grilled onions, sweet peppers, and tomatoes. Organic mixed green salads always come with papaya seed dressing. To remind us that they're Brazilians, every couple of weeks they put out their version of the classic *muqueca*, typically a stew of fish, palm oil, coconut, and spices, but here served as chunks of fish in a *muqueca* sauce sitting on the plate next to a couple of scoops of rice (what's a meal in Hawai'i without scoops of rice?). They also carry that buzz-inducing Brazilian soft drink—*guaraná*.

Bottom Line: Lots of fresh air, seafood, and salad between sets at Pipeline and Sunset.

71

TED'S BAKERY

59-024 Kamehameha Hwy. • 638-8207
7 a.m.-6 p.m. daily
BYOB? Yes • Credit cards? Yes
per person: $3-$5

Disappointment—that's the word, the sinking feeling you get, when you walk into Ted's at Sunset Beach and find they're out of chocolate *haupia* cream pie. They make over one thousand of them each week, but hotels, markets, and restaurants throughout the islands love 'em too, so you've got to be quick—or at least early. In the nearly fifty years since Ted Nakamura's parents opened their mom and pop market on Kamehameha Highway just Kahuku of Sunset, things have changed a lot in the neighborhood. Surfing has become a big deal, and Sunset Beach, Banzai Pipeline, and Velzyland are just minutes away. Ted's has changed too, and the market is no more, but the repute of Ted and his pastries has spread. You can order hot food items, such as plate lunches, breakfast, or sandwiches, and they've recently set tables and umbrellas out front. But the most popular breakfast items, omelets, are no better than okay, the loco moco isn't the best around, and the popular teriyaki and mahimahi plates are really just so-so, although homemade corned beef hash is a standout. Mainly, the surfing crowd likes it because it's cheap. Having said that, just about anything connected with baking is well worth ordering. The croissant breakfast sandwich, filled with egg, cheese, and bacon is good—but it's because of the croissant. The hot dog bun is also a winner—but that's because of the rich pastry around the dog. They also sell plenty of giant chocolate éclairs, plus cinnamon rolls, glazed donuts, and chiffon pies. Me, more than once I've eaten half a chocolate *haupia* cream pie at one sitting.

Bottom Line: Stick with the pastries and you'll get some of the island's best calories.

72

Francis Barbecue Chicken

Sugar Mill yard • 271-2045
Saturday–Sunday 7 a.m.-6 p.m.
BYOB? No • Credit cards? No
per person: $4

Norma Cristobal puts out a mean barbecued chicken. That's the first thing to know about this real neighborhood spot that for nearly a dozen years was out on Farrington Highway before moving recently into Waialua town to the old sugar mill just off the corner of Goodale Avenue and Kealohanui Street. The second thing is that she's open only on weekends. On Saturdays and Sundays, from blocks away you'll see a plume of smoke from the large grill. When you get there, you'll see that the sign over the grill, in addition to promoting chicken, also advertises *lechon,* but you can get that only in a whole pig–size portion, which makes it not so handy for most of us. Anyhow, the chicken—which we'd call *huli huli* except that Norma says that's a trademarked name as far as its commercial use is concerned—is the best: succulent, moist, beautifully crisp skin and not too salty. She dishes it off the grill while she's stoking the *kiawe* coals with wood from several wheelbarrows parked out front. The flavor is pepper and salt and paprika and some other spices she won't go into, and the spitted birds get turned and moved around the grill often enough so that they're cooked evenly. On the three outside picnic tables under a canvas cover nearby are bottles of Tabasco, *shoyu,* and both sweet and hot Thai chili sauces. The only other edible you'll usually see with the 300 or so chickens roasted every weekend is rice, but occasionally Norma will have some fresh corn on the cob. Dessert is homemade buttered *mochi* bars, coconut flavor, nice and chewy.

Bottom Line: Tender, crispy, delicious *kiawe*-grilled chicken two days a week.

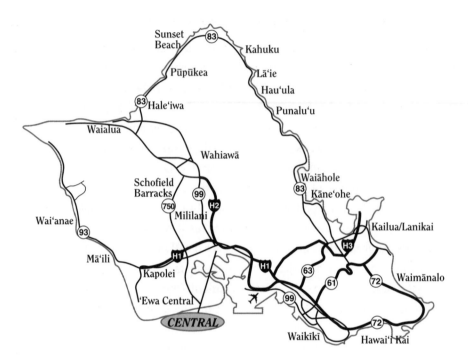

CENTRAL

'Aiea
Cuu Long
Forty Niner

Mililani
Loco Moco Drive Inn
Mililani Drive Inn

Salt Lake
Mark's Drive Inn
Royal Palace Chinese Restaurant

Wahiawā
Shige's Saimin Stand
Sunny Side

Waimalu
Chun Wah Kam Noodle Factory
Shiro's

Waipahu
Elena's
Highway Inn
Kristen's Kitchen
Tanioka's Seafoods & Catering

CUU LONG

98-199 Kamehameha Hwy. • 488-6041
daily 10 a.m.-10 p.m.
BYOB? Yes • Credit cards? Yes
per person: $6-$8

Potted plants, high ceilings, battered white tables and chairs—and *phô* bowls. Everywhere you look, bowls of the steaming, flavorful broth. No table, it seems, is without its large ceramic bowl of the traditional Vietnamese soup. It's like part of the decor. Not that the simple menu doesn't list—even feature—other dishes, such as salads, appetizers, and rice. But he who enters here seemingly cannot ignore the soup. Admittedly, the *phô* in the storefront restaurant inside the Pearl Kai Shopping Center behind Tower Records is one of the best. Whether you add meatballs or fatty brisket, eye round or sirloin, or just the accompanying herbs and greens with *shoyu* or chili sauce, they're serving one of the most satisfying dishes in the neighborhood. If you don't believe it, just watch the steady flow of customers from midmorning on. But there's also room on the table for those who need more than soup to walk out feeling they've eaten well. Green papaya salad comes with shrimp and slices of boiled pork and green papaya, mint leaves, and ground peanuts, the dressing on the side making it mildly spicy. And a chicken dish sautéed in lemongrass and onions, with fresh cucumber, daikon, carrots, and tomatoes on the side is refreshing. The most attractive item on the bill of fare besides *phô* is the barbecued pork chop, although it's not really barbecued, no matter what the menu says, but pan-fried: two large, thin chops that come to the table crispy and exceptionally flavorful, very nicely cooked.

Bottom Line: One of the better bowls of *phô*, plus a handful of other tasty dishes.

FORTY NINER

98-110 Honomanū St. • no telephone
open Wednesday–Monday 9 a.m.-4 p.m.
BYOB? No • Credit cards? No
per person: $3-$6

I'd always been intrigued by the small, nondescript creamy brown building standing by itself above the road where Honomanū Street comes down from 'Aiea Heights to meet Kamehameha Highway. Don't know why, maybe the name, Forty Niner. When I finally started to drop in from time to time to try the food, it turned out no one really knew the name's origin, except they were certain it didn't come from the San Francisco football team. Brothers Richard—he's still behind the stove—and Henry Chigami have aged along with the business, first started almost sixty years ago by their parents as a lunchwagon on the corner lot, before the "kids" built the building, ten counter stools and a room in the back with several tables that seems like a family room in someone's house. They stayed with a really simple menu, and have been dishing it out all these years. To make it even simpler, Richard and Henry elected not to have a telephone. "We wouldn't be able to keep up with the takeout." Now, there's a real problem for you. *Saimin*, in large or small bowls, is the menu's mainstay; they make their own *dashi* each morning, into which go noodles, fish cake, *char siu* and green onions. It's a broth with which you won't go wrong. There's a substantial list of hamburgers—homemade patties with cheese and/or egg—the deluxe model adding grilled onions and pickles. The only items that aren't soup, sandwiches, or breakfast eggs and meats are the beef cutlet—thin slices of roast beef floating in gravy—and hamburger steak, homemade. Nice and simple, and all that sunlight flooding in through the large windows.

Bottom Line: Been there forever, serving much better than average *saimin*, with a choice of hamburgers and sandwiches.

Loco Moco Drive Inn

95-1249 Mehe'ula Parkway • 625-8778
Monday–Thursday 9:30 a.m.-9 p.m.
Friday–Saturday 9:30 a.m.-10 p.m., Sunday 9:30 a.m.-8 p.m.
BYOB? No • Credit cards? No
per person: $3-$6

Don't be fooled by the handful of "light" dishes on the menu—*saimin,* grilled mahimahi, tossed salad, even a garden burger. The menu is mostly crunch, the best dishes heavily breaded and deliciously deep-fried; when you get up to leave, the table's littered with crumbs. We're talking a group of five clean-cut plate lunch restaurants (I particularly like the one in the middle of Mililani Town Center, which has been there since 1993, but others are in Waipahu, 'Ewa Beach, Hawai'i Kai, and Kapolei) with small, wood-trimmed Formica tables seating maybe two dozen people, and a constant flow in the takeout line. The biggest-selling plates are chicken, and there's lots of it: fried, barbecue, *katsu,* lemon, orange, or *mochiko,* but variety plates, like the seafood combo of mahimahi, shrimp, and a choice of short ribs, chicken, teriyaki "steak" (the usual thin-sliced teriyaki beef) or teriyaki pork are good value and good flavor. Scoops of rice and macaroni salad, naturally, which reminds me that this mac salad has a tiny spicy kick to it—a nice change from the usual bland version. They're not chintzy on quantity, especially in the sandwiches; the chicken *katsu,* for example, comes with two large pieces of crispy bird. And where else, even in the islands, can you get a sandwich (grilled cheese or fried egg) for $1.29? Well, you might want to add $.45 and get it "deluxe."

Bottom Line: Crispy, flavorful fried plate lunches in a clean atmosphere with good value.

MILILANI DRIVE INN

95-026 Kamehameha Hwy. • 623-2268
daily 10 a.m.-10 p.m.
BYOB? No • Credit cards? No
per person: $3-$6

Nearly forty thousand people live in Mililani, but when the developers master-planned and built the neighborhood, they seemed to forget we're in Hawai'i and didn't leave much room for local food. Burger Kings and Starbucks, yes, but holes-in-the-wall? A mere handful. One of these is in an obscure location behind the Freedom service station next to Mililani Center on Kamehameha Highway, a small store with a few tables inside and out, refrigerator and ice-maker in the seating area, and the usual extensive menu board (I continually wonder how these tiny places can have such large menus, serve such decent food at such low prices, and still make money). The stream of customers is thin but steady: a worker taking a midmorning break in a corner booth, his legs tucked up under him while he scarfs down loco moco, a kid coming in to pick up his mother's lunch, a retired resident living nearby taking her time over an order of fried rice. Garlic chicken and *katsu* seem to be the dishes of choice. The chicken is interestingly prepared in dark meat strips, with lots of fried garlic and green onions, served on a bed of cabbage. Ditto the mahimahi, thin pieces tenderly cooked. Shrimp *katsu*, although obviously frozen, is a satisfying dish, while the house fried rice is often served with its own chicken *katsu*, even if they do forgo green onions. Last but not least is an occasional special, homemade spring rolls, well worth ordering.

Bottom Line: Decent local food hidden on the edge of suburbia.

MARK'S DRIVE INN

4510 Salt Lake Blvd. • 488-6796
daily 10 a.m.-9 p.m.
BYOB? Yes • Credit cards? No
per person: $3-$5

In the mid-afternoons, when things have slowed down, Mark Wong's young waitresses often sit down at a table in front and kill the time making pot stickers. Walking in and seeing this immediately makes me want to start out with these tasty morsels, always delicious and bursting with flavor. No different than most of the other dishes in Wong's small—eighteen seats—store on the corner of a building in the Ice Palace parking lot. The list of appetizing foods in the usual large portions (although many dishes do come in both mini and large sizes) is extensive, but it really comes down to three delectable categories: fried noodles, stir-fries, and plate lunches. They're all worth filling up on, but the *mochiko* chicken is one of the best, nicely breaded and cooked perfectly. And though they're big on mahimahi and shrimp dishes, they especially love chicken here—I once counted twenty variations on the menu. Maybe it's the stir-fried chicken with mushrooms that's most popular, a major dish, overflowing with mushrooms, chicken, and onions. Pork chops are also a favorite, the one many like best being the house pork chop, a big, thin chop lathered with teriyaki gravy and tons of lightly cooked onions. The plate lunches come not only with the usual rice and macaroni salad, but also with two other vegetables. Added bonuses? Real waitress service and real dishes on which to enjoy Wong's fine food.

Bottom Line: The best in well-prepared fried noodles, stir-fries, and plate lunches.

ROYAL PALACE CHINESE RESTAURANT

4510 Salt Lake Blvd. • 487-6662
10:30 a.m.-9 p.m.
BYOB? Yes • Credit cards? Yes
per person: $6-$11

People love it and for years now it's had a reputation. Partly because of excellent value on the menu, partly because of the good food. Not a bad combination. Gourmet it is not, but there's quality in the standard dishes—mostly Cantonese—and a handful of intriguing recipes you don't see too often on otherwise similar menus. Tucked in close to the freeway near Aloha Stadium, Royal Palace is in the same complex that hosts the Ice Palace, in a location just a bit tricky to access. The L-shaped room is filled with mostly round, family-style tables, the kind of dining room where a regular on his way out, seeing that you're ready to order, might stop and say, "I hope you ate bread and water for three days before you came." You want to be hungry when you come in, is the implication, and he's usually talking about the midday buffet, one of the better Chinese lines around. But even single dishes from the menu can be meals in themselves. Best to share, of course, the more the better. Might want to include an easy dish, like beef *chow fun* with *choy sum*, and crispy roast duck is certainly worth ordering. A plate of sweet-and-sour fish fillet comes gently fried, the sauce loaded with vegetables. Vegetables here, by the way, are excellent, whether stir-fried or steamed. Less common dishes also worth ordering are ones such as *mui choy kay yuk*—pork that is long-braised and fat and rich—or cold chicken in ginger sauce, perfectly poached.

Bottom Line: Better-than-average Chinese dining at good prices, with a few unexpectedly interesting dishes on the menu.

SHIGE'S SAIMIN STAND

70 Kukui St. • 621-3621
Monday–Thursday 10 a.m.-10 p.m.
Friday–Saturday 10 a.m.-midnight
BYOB? Yes • Credit cards? No
per person: $3-$6

I don't care what the sign says, this is no "stand." It's a bright, modern restaurant at the far end of a strip of stores on the north end of Wahiawā, and it has deservedly made a name for itself by keeping things simple and doing them well. They also serve a limited selection of plate lunches and some sandwiches—any of the three sizes in juicy hamburgers is worth ordering—but mostly it's broth. The large bowls of hot, savory soups from which customers at the seven-seat counter or the spread-out tables are slurping come in two forms: the house staple, *saimin,* and *wunton* or *wunton mein.* The *dashi* isn't homemade here, but they're hell on wheels with their homemade noodles, using a recipe and technique passed down from Ross Shigeoka's grandfather, flat noodles instead of the more customary round kind. In the *saimin* you've got noodles, *char siu*, Spam, green onions, strips of fried egg, and fish cake. There's also a vegetarian bowl of soup available. Add a dash of Tabasco, *shoyu,* or chile pepper and you've got a heck of a meal. When Shigeoka set up shop in 1990 he'd never been in the restaurant business before, but with Grandpa's recipe and lots of family help—sisters and nephews still work the kitchen, counter, and tables, perhaps accounting for the unusually good service—the citizens must have liked it because a few years back Shigeoka doubled the size of the store. Not bad for Grandpa's noodles and some broth.

Bottom Line: Appetizing bowls of *saimin* well served in an easy setting.

SUNNY SIDE

1017 Kilani Ave. • 621-7188
Monday–Friday 6 a.m.-6 p.m., Saturday 6 a.m.-4 p.m.
BYOB? No • Credit cards? No
per person: $3-$5

Locals—and they're about all you'll find at this back street Wahiawā locale—clear their own tables when they're finished and don't need to inquire about where the coffeemaker is in order to refill their cups. That's how it goes at Lucy Shimonishi's place, which her family has run since 1977 and whose main reputation is for its pies. But Lucy's is also a pretty good spot to latch on to a flavorsome meal at a better than good price. Although it's easy to miss driving by, what you won't miss is the line in front at the outside takeout window, where those who are not "in the know" may be bemoaning the fact that, by ten in the morning, a favorite pie, like the chocolate cream, is likely to be sold out. Inside the nondescript room, which seats maybe forty, you order through a large window, looking into the kitchen where a half dozen staff are always on the move, and where Lucy isn't always the only family member at work. A big morning seller is the fried rice special, served with eggs and a hot dog, a really good version of this dish for at least two reasons—its large amount of crispy fried ham, and the fried onions mixed in. Looking around the room you'll notice that egg servings are always perfectly done. If it's lunch—or even breakfast—Sunny Side dishes up a better-than-you'd-expect hamburger, moist and juicy because the patty is homemade, and there's plenty of ketchup, mayonnaise, and lettuce aboard.

Bottom Line: Decent food at a very good value in a very local place.

CHUN WAH KAM NOODLE FACTORY

98-040 Kamehameha Hwy. • 485-1107
Monday–Tuesday 7:30 a.m.-7 p.m., Wednesday–Friday 7:30 a.m.-
8:30 p.m., Saturday 8:30 a.m.-8:30 p.m., Sunday 6:30 a.m.-4 p.m.
BYOB? No • Credit cards? Yes
per person: $4-$6

They hit you coming in the door, those mouth-watering aromas—steaming buns and garlic, hoisin sauce and curries, roasting
meats and Chinese spices. But if you're thinking the usual neighborhood *manapua* shop, forget it. They're high-tech here. Makes
you think he'd have had a hard time, the old man, envisioning it all
when he opened his tiny takeout shop in Honolulu's industrial area
over sixty-two years ago. That Kalihi original's still there, but his
kid, Nelson Chun, has taken things so much farther in ʻAiea, from
the modern storefront that stands out over the multitude of other
food purveyors in the Waimalu Shopping Center to the big stain-
less steel kitchen you can see in the back. The dining area is bright
blond seating and an array of steam tables with nearly three dozen
entrées. But first, the buns: baked hot dog snuggled in its fresh,
doughy pastry shell; roast duck *manapua* crammed with meat,
onion, five-spice powder, and hoisin sauce; garlic chicken *manapua* bursting with the tastes of mushrooms, chicken, and garlic;
crispy *gau gee,* handy for a quick snack on the way home.
Customers, often with number in hand, get good browsing as they
wait their turn while large paper boxes are being filled with food:
sweet-and-sour cabbage with pork slices; delicious pork with
ground eggplant, slightly spicy. And noodles, half a dozen vari-
eties—chow mein, *chow fun*, udon, take your pick. But, although
garlic is much of what it's all about here, don't bother with garlic
chicken, a dish with lots of garlic and lots of cooking—too much
cooking.

Bottom Line: Outstanding *manapua* plus a variety of appetizing
dishes to go with it.

SHIRO'S

98-020 Kamehameha Hwy. • 488-4834
Monday–Thursday 7 a.m.-10:30 p.m.
Friday–Saturday 7 a.m.-11:30 p.m., Sunday 7 a.m.-10:30 p.m.
BYOB? No • Credit cards? No
per person $4-$7

Shiro Matsuo's restaurant tables are nearly always crowded with big bowls full of broth, making you want to dive into the steaming, comforting bowls as soon as you walk in. And even if I'm not sure I'd agree with Matsuo when he calls his four restaurants ('Ewa Beach, Waipahu, Waimalu, and Kalihi) "an *adventure* in *saimin* dining," he's certainly developed a menu since he opened the first spot thirty-eight years ago. While adults are "adventuring" with the bill of fare, kids get paper placemats and crayons. And even if it's not exactly an adventure, it is a huge selection, with so many *saimins* (sixty) that even regulars order by the number. The big favorite is giant number 58, *dodonpa,* packed with ten garnishes, including roast beef, *char siu,* egg roll, *wun tun,* luncheon meat, mushrooms, and vegetables, with a large shrimp tempura and tartar sauce on the side. Menu number 15, shrimp tempura *saimin,* is a close second in popularity, the shrimp sharing the bowl with piles of noodles and *wun tun.* The key to any *saimin,* of course, is the *dashi,* and this one is rich, made from scratch, and, as the menu brags, "fresh" and "raw." French fries are ordered by perhaps half the tables, whether it's breakfast, lunch, or dinner, and if you're not ordering *saimin*—or even if you are—then the best bet is the country fried noodles. There's also a substantial breakfast menu of sandwiches and plate lunches.

Bottom Line: Huge selection of good broth and lots of garnishes in family-friendly restaurants.

ELENA'S

94-300 Farrington Hwy. • 671-3279
Sunday–Thursday 5 a.m.-8:45 p.m.
Friday–Saturday 5 a.m.-9 p.m.
BYOB? Yes • Credit cards? Yes
per person: $4-$9

ISLAND OF OʻAHU • CENTRAL • WAIPAHU

Delicate diners, you'd think, would avoid this address. But the neighborhood ladies, attired in muumuus and woven hats, are in and out all day: they appreciate good food. For thirty years island aficionados have known you can't go wrong no matter what you order in Theo and Elena Butuyan's place, especially in the current location just off Farrington Highway in front of Pacific Supermarket. You get that "this is going to be good" feeling as soon as you walk in the door, hearing the Tagalog conversations throughout the room, and with a big, appetizing, freshly roasted *lechon* displayed to catch the eye. As good as that *lechon* looks, that's how good the rest of the dishes on the menu taste. You just might find yourself sharing a table in the small front room (there's a larger room in back). Next to you is a woman, arms draped with gold jewelry, just digging into a plate that has the largest omelet on it you've ever seen, enough to feed three people, smelling of garlic and stuffed with tender, long-cooked pork adobo and fried rice. She obviously loves every bite, and when your own hot bowl of *sari-sari* comes, it's just as good, a fabulous dish of flavorful broth, eggplant, squash, long beans, and crispy pork. Then there's a large platter heaped with *pansit*, rich with pork and vegetables. But the dish to die for—at least one of them—is shrimp *sarciado*, the shellfish sautéed with tomato, onion, and egg, wonderfully flavorful, the sauce nearly creamy. We can get earthier here, with deep-fried intestines, or pork in blood sauce, but why push our luck?

Bottom Line: Delicious food, huge portions, and reasonable prices make this maybe the Number One Filipino restaurant on the island.

HIGHWAY INN

94-226 Leokū St. • 677-4345
Monday–Saturday 9 a.m.-2 p.m., 5 p.m.-8 p.m.
Sunday 11 a.m.-2 p.m.
BYOB? No • Credit cards? Yes
per person: $4-$9

Let's just call this a Tale of Two Menus. We're talking the Hawaiian Menu and the American Menu, although, if you're a first-timer, a waitress like JoAnn might laughingly insist, "If you're here the first time, you have to order Hawaiian, it's so good." And much of it is, in this old storefront restaurant off Farrington Highway on the west edge of Waipahu in a nondescript storefront behind a Longs Drugstore. It's the third location for the Highway Inn since its inception over fifty years ago. Today, the Inn seats about three dozen diners on old red vinyl chairs under a stained ceiling, and at least a handful always seem to be friends or family, sitting around laughing, talking—and eating. And yeah, there is an American menu, of items such as pork chops, hamburgers, and egg and meat breakfasts, but it's the Hawaiian side that calls for attention. They make it all on the premises, the most popular of the local dishes probably being the stew, thick and savory and flavorful with beef, tripe, or *na'au pua'a*. But strips of *pipikaula* are awfully tasty and so is pork *laulau*. The dishes are served on those old cafeteria-style trays we used to eat from in elementary school. But perhaps it's the little things that the restaurant does best: the *haupia* is absolutely fabulous, and don't you just love the tiny plates of fresh onion slices to dip into the Hawaiian salt or chile water?

Bottom Line: Good Hawaiian in a restaurant where locals appreciate it.

KRISTEN'S KITCHEN

94-801D Farrington Hwy. • 678-2529
Monday–Friday 9 a.m.-8 p.m., Saturday–Sunday 8 a.m.-2:30 p.m.
BYOB? No • Credit cards? No
per person: $4-$6

Filipo Elisala says if he knew then what he knows now about the difficulties of running a restaurant, he'd never have bought the place six years ago. But with no previous experience in the restaurant business he's still there, in the kitchen much of the time, serving dozens of breakfasts, tons of plate lunches, and, surprisingly, a small menu of flavorsome and modestly priced Italian dishes; the platesful of linguini and baby clams or pasta *amatriciana* are remnants of a departed gourmet-type chef from Honolulu. Elisala's small restaurant with its six vinyl booths in a strip of stores on Farrington Highway in Waipahu is busiest at lunch. As a regular lunch customer says, "It's pretty good, eh?" Could be, because they do serve an appetizing spicy calamari stir-fry, which sometimes isn't as spicy as it might be but is appealingly packed with broccoli, zucchini, bell peppers, and onions. The macaroni and potato salad might be the best on the highway, and the lemon chicken *katsu*, with a sweetish lemon dipping sauce on the side, has a crisp, crunchy coating. Breakfast is a fairly simple affair, the most popular dish being Kristen's Special, an omelet of fresh spinach, mushrooms, and ground beef, sort of what they call Diamond Jim's Special in some other parts of the country.

Bottom Line: The customers are right, it's "pretty good," especially if you choose the right plates.

TANIOKA'S SEAFOODS & CATERING

94-903 Farrington Hwy. • 671-3779
Monday–Friday 9 a.m.-6 p.m., Saturday 9 a.m.-5 p.m.,
Sunday 9 a.m.-3 p.m.
BYOB? No • Credit cards? Yes
per person: $5-$10

If you like what Hawai'i's cooks can do with raw seafood, being in Tanioka's is likely to make you feel like a kid in a candy store: you can't decide what to choose. There's so much going on in the takeout-only store on Farrington Highway next to a 7-11 market that while you're figuring out what to order, it's all you can do to stay on your feet in the constant throng of customers going in and out. Whether you're on your way home, going to work, or off to the beach, this is a Numbah One stop. Over twenty kinds of *poke* crowd the display cases; you just want to try each one. Biggest sellers are the tasty *limu* or onion recipes, but smoked *'ahi poke* goes out the door in big quantities, and so does the "original" dried *poke,* all of it beautifully fresh—this is not a place that smells like fish. But there's more. Although the concentration is fish, the menu ranges from fried chicken to tempura, from small trays of sashimi to tasty fish cakes, from succulent *tako* to a variety of some of the best bentos around, from *laulau* to *musubi,* from *maki* to both large and small cone sushi. It's all been going on since they opened in 1978, and although I can't say I've eaten everything in sight, if you've never tried Tanioka's slightly spicy Japanese clams, you've got a treat coming. Or wasabi miso *tako,* or just the standard onion *poke* or . . . . I could go on, but I might forget to pick up a couple of bags of goodies from their giant selection of Hawaiian candies.

Bottom Line: Outstanding fresh seafoods, and more, for picnics, office, or home—and they'll be glad (have I got the right word here?) to drop off a funeral catering menu.

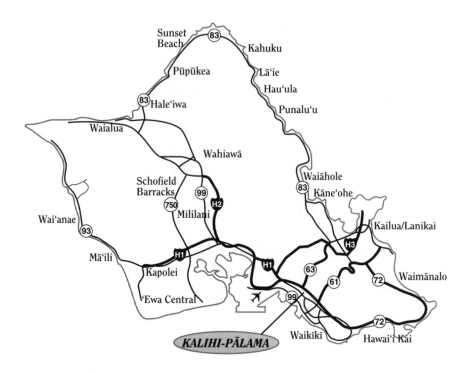

KALIHI-PĀLAMA

Kalihi
Helena's Hawaiian Foods
Leong's Cafe
Mokauea Mart
Ray's Cafe

Kapālama
Bob's Bar-B-Que
Ethel's Grill
Fat Boy's Local Drive-In
Yohei Sushi

Liliha
Liliha Bakery and Coffee Shop
New Uptown Fountain

Pālama
Kapiolani Coffee Shop (Kam Bowl)
Mitsu-Ken Okazu and Catering
Yuki's

Sand Island
La Mariana Sailing Club, Inc.

HELENA'S HAWAIIAN FOODS

1240 N. School St. • 845-8044
Tuesday–Friday 10 a.m.-7:30 p.m.
BYOB? No • Credit cards? No
per person: $5-$9

Helena Chock is a story. Eighty-seven, she's still at the cash register, although grandson Craig has replaced her as cook, and a few years ago her Hawaiian restaurant became one of only a handful to receive the prestigious James Beard Foundation "Regional Classic" award. Not bad for a fifty-eight-year-old School Street joint (moved four years ago from a different location), whose tables look as though they've been picked up at various thrift shops—even if the chairs do match. Family is still all over the place, serving the same menu that's become a local classic over the years. No sandwiches, no breakfast, no loco moco, no Portuguese sausage, just pure Hawaiian. Poi of course, and on the complimentary side with each meal are tiny dishes of onions and salt, and *haupia*. At first glance, menu prices appear to be distinctly on the low side, but, although the bill is unlikely ever to run very high, portions are small and a real Hawaiian eater is likely to want two dishes, even three or four. Nearly everyone, at one time or another, orders short ribs *pipikaula* style, meaty and cut fairly thick. Luau squid is coconut-sweet, with slices of tentacle mixed in, and Helena's *poke*—usually *ʻahi*—mixed with *ʻopihi* is a salty, crunchy dish you don't run into all that often, as is butterfish collar, either fried or boiled, the latter served either plain or with gravy. *Laulau* is on the small side, overflowing its plate, but packed with nearly as much pork as its larger competitors.

Bottom Line: One of Oʻahu's important traditional Hawaiian restaurants, plus Sunflower brand chocolate chip cookies at the cash register.

LEONG'S CAFE

★
Da Bes'

2343 N. King St. • 845-0301
Monday–Wednesday 10 a.m.-2 p.m.,
Thursday–Friday 10 a.m.-7:30 p.m.
BYOB? Yes ("as long as they behave themselves") • Credit cards? No
per person: $5-$8

At least a couple of other spots have bigger reputations in Hawaiian food, but for my money Leong's is at least as good—maybe better. Parking is lousy, and don't bother showing up on weekends, because they don't. But since 1950, when Lucy Leong began cooking breakfast and lunch for stevedores on their way to work—moving to the current location in 1966—this has been a destination for those who know good local food, from local politicians to gourmet chefs. The room has high ceilings, long plastic tables, commercial fans, pictures of old Hawai'i on the walls, and lots of clatter from the pots and pans back in the kitchen. The menu? It's a simple one. The *laulau*, for example, is just okay, perhaps because Debbie Leong, Lucy's daughter-in-law who's been there since well before Lucy died in 1997, doesn't always make her own. But the *kālua* pig makes visitors see why we like the dish so much, and *pipikaula* is popular with just about anyone who comes in. Both *lomi* salmon and chicken long rice often sell out early. Debbie uses top sirloin for some of the meat dishes, which may be one reason why the chopsteak and onions is so *'ono*! Then there's luscious luau beef stew, its hot bowls filled to overflowing with taro leaf and meat, and squid luau, with the sweet taste of coconut milk. Those stews are worth the trip themselves.

Bottom Line: Could be the best Hawaiian food on the island.

Mokauea Mart

Island of Oʻahu • Kalihi-Pālama • Kalihi

Confused—that's probably an apt description of the first-time customer who walks through the door of this small market in a shabby, mixed–residential-commercial neighborhood a block *mauka* of Nimitz Highway. If it weren't for a couple of guys hunched over plates of ham, Portuguese sausage, eggs, rice, and macaroni salad at a six-seat table on the left as you walk in, you'd wonder if you were in the right place. No menu at all, not even on the wall, although the "Sashimi, Poke" sign on the front of the building might be a hint. On the other side of the table are three hot plates—another good sign if you want to eat in instead of just grabbing a packaged sandwich from the rear wall. Asking what's to eat is like an American tourist trying to order breakfast in a back street bistro in Seoul: proprietor Nam Sok Cho, charming as she is, boasts only limited English. Still, the limited hot food selection she added five years ago when she bought the small neighborhood market is good value. The eggs are always done well, best flavored with chopstick pickings from the bowls of kim chee that are always on the table. And if you're around at midmorning, your dining companion may well be the proprietor—if she's not busy making an order of *ʻahi poke*. I've noticed that at least once the fish was still frozen as Sok Cho prepared it, so I'd pass on that dish, as I would on another choice from the spoken menu, *saimin*, the packaged variety.

Bottom Line: Good, quick stop for eggs and kim chee.

RAY'S CAFE

Da Bes'

2033 N. King St. • 841-2771
Monday–Saturday 5 a.m.-8:30 p.m., Sunday 5 a.m.-2 p.m.
BYOB? Yes • Credit cards? No
per person: $3-$9

Standing on the sidewalk outside Ray's faded storefront in Kalihi half a block off Gulick means you're waiting for one of three things: your takeout order, a table, or a bus. It's too small to wait inside. Just twenty seats in this grubby little meat palace. Decor? What decor? Not much different in this location where he's been now for four years than it was in the earlier years down in Chinatown for Felix Pintor, who named the place after his son— who's now twenty-three years old. It's the grill we're talking about here, and the meat, and the portions. "Pretty good for the price," as one regular says, and he really hasn't given Ray's its due. This is not Prime grade meat we're talking about, but it's darned good. And everything is cooked just right, whether it's soft scrambled eggs with a smoky, medium-rare New York steak, grilled pork chops, butterfish, or *ono*. The single waiter spends his days hustling through the room, setting big portions down on the table next to commercial-sized bottles of salad dressings and ketchup. A thick prime rib oozes flavor, just like the rib, sirloin, or T-bone steaks. At breakfast—a favorite meal here—omelets overflow the plate, and the Portuguese sweet bread French toast is among the best in town. Regulars, for good reason, love everything about this small restaurant except, they say, if the door is open, as it usually is, and it's windy, "hold on to your napkin."

Bottom Line: Maybe the best red meat value in town.

Bob's Bar-B-Que

1366 Dillingham Blvd. • 842-3663
Monday–Thursday 6 a.m.-10 p.m.
Friday–Saturday 6 a.m.-11 p.m., Sunday 7:30 a.m.-10 p.m.
BYOB? No • Credit cards? No
per person: $4-$10

These might be the best barbecued beef ribs in town, meaty, dripping with fat, and falling off the bone in their sweet, gooey sauce. If they'd been on the menu twenty-eight years ago, when Bob and Marcia Wong first opened their joint at the busy Dillingham-Waiakamilo corner in Kapālama, things would have been simpler. The takeout spaghetti stand the couple first opened didn't make it, so they changed course, and one of the things they added was a smoker. Today, at the asphalt corner edged with shaded outdoor tables, their kitchen is one of the busiest around. The BBQ super combo looks expensive on the menu (we're talking Hawaiʻi plates here) but as soon as you heft it, you realize you're talking a meal for two, or three. Comes with those beef ribs, plus baby back pork ribs in the same sauce, and *kal bi* short ribs, which are pretty good themselves. Then there's tasty teri beef, teri chicken, which is just okay, three scoops rice, and two of an undistinguished macaroni salad. Their deluxe sandwiches are well worth ordering, on soft, fresh buns, although I'd go for the teri pork over the slabs of chicken. You just can't have mainland-type barbecue without beans, and Bob's baked beans are okay, an unusual mixture of kidneys, limas, and garbanzos, served just a little bit firm. Bob's is, justly, famed for its rich malts, thick enough that they have to be eaten rather than drunk.

Bottom Line: Excellent mainland-type barbecue side by side with local-style and good malts.

ETHEL'S GRILL

Da Bes'

232 Kalihi St. • 847-6467
Monday–Saturday 6 a.m.-1 p.m.
BYOB? Yes • Credit cards? No
per person: $3-$6

Yeah, it's grubby and sticky and seats maybe two dozen people, and parking can be impossible in the high-density location *makai* of Nimitz Highway. But for twenty-seven years Taisho and Ethel Ishii have been dishing out their exceptionally well prepared local food to customers flocking from all over the city. Ethel herself most often works the front of the crowded room—whose walls are plastered with sumo photographs—hustling steaming plates and bowls out to her customers, while Taisho does the cooking. Many of the recipes are hers, a handful being dishes you won't find any-place else in town. Like the "secret" sauce that makes *tataki* sashi-mi one of the most popular dishes (hint: it's got mushrooms). But *sashimi* you can get anyplace. What you might not get just any-place is a plate of *ume* chicken—rolled chicken breast stuffed with *ume,* wrapped in nori, breaded, and then fried. A truly unique fla-vor. A couple of other popular choices are more conventional, but especially well prepared. The *oyako donburi,* filled with egg, rice, chicken, vegetables, and tofu, is darned good, as is *gyoza min,* served in a giant ceramic bowl steaming with dumplings and a par-ticularly flavorful broth, with cilantro, noodles, and *kai choy.* All the plates come with miso soup, a green salad, and a drink. Portions are large, but if—God forbid—you want 'em even larger, there's a two dollar charge for "sumo size."

Bottom Line: It's all the best, with fine value and some adventures for the curious palate.

ISLAND OF OʻAHU • KALIHI-PĀLAMA • KAPĀLAMA

FAT BOY'S LOCAL DRIVE-IN

2018 Republican St. • 841-2697
Monday–Saturday 9:30 a.m.-2 p.m.
BYOB? Yes • Credit cards? No
per person: $4-$6

When Carroll Ung opened up in a difficult industrial location five years ago, he thought he'd serve local food with a twist. He'd dish up the usual stuff—teriyaki, Spam, hot dog, and so on. But he'd also lace the menu with just a bit of what he calls "gourmet" overtones. The little place he opened behind a used car lot just off Nimitz Highway and Puʻuhale Road is hard to get into, and parking is a bitch. But if the lines at the counter from midmorning on are any indication—and they certainly are—the joint with twelve seats and stacks of supplies in every corner does a great job. Ung opens later than you'd expect for an industrial location, so even though there is a breakfast menu, the emphasis is clearly on lunch, and on the lunch menu the emphasis is dramatically on chicken. Their excellent garlic and sesame chicken is everywhere: on the plate lunches, in the bentos, and in the hearts and the order-line chatter of the clientele. It's first-rate: deep-fried with the skin on, not cooked too long and with a slightly sweet tang. Besides the usual list of plate lunches, always look carefully at the list of specials, where something like grilled *ono* in a creamy onion pesto sauce is to salivate over. They're close to the airport, so stopping for a bento on the way to catch a plane can make you the envy—or the bane— of your seatmates. Fat Boy's bento covers most of the local bases, complete with chicken, teri beef, mahimahi, hot dog, and Spam. Did I mention rice? Do I have to?

Bottom Line: Nifty little spot by Sand Island with outstanding garlic sesame chicken and delicious seafood specials.

YOHEI SUSHI

1111 Dillingham Blvd. • 841-3773
Monday–Saturday, 11 a.m.-1:45 p.m., 5 p.m.-9:30 p.m.
BYOB? No • Credit cards? Yes
per person: $12-$35

To dip or not to dip, that is the question. Because unless you're a connoisseur you might just forget that, in the world of sushi, not everything needs to be dipped in *shoyu*. And since the most appetizing way to enjoy what may be Honolulu's finest sushi is to put yourself in the hands of the sushi chef, it's only fair that, with a nod of his head, he's the guy to say when to dip. The small, bald guy next to you, slouched on a corner stool, obviously knows when to dip. "Leave it up to him," he nods toward the chef. "I just got back from Japan, and these guys are better." And, one dish after another, you'll find he must be right. The place itself, hidden in a multiuse complex on Kokea at Dillingham, has simple decor, with low ceilings, waitresses in white smocks, and quiet Japanese music in the background. No smells of fish here, unless you count the luscious aroma of sizzling seafood from the small gas grill behind the sushi bar. Selections might include *hamachi* with miso and scallions; seared and seasoned *'ahi*; scallops marinated in *shoyu* then seared and wrapped in nori; tuna with raw quail eggs, pickled vegetables, shaved bonito, and mint leaf; salmon with salmon eggs and yam sprouts. There's more than sushi on the menu, which also boasts soba and udon noodle dishes, and tempura and bento, any of which is excellent. And they do have it on the menu, but "California roll?" The young sushi chef claims owner Kazuto Obara "doesn't really believe in it."

Bottom Line: Outstanding sushi, both simple and creative, maybe the best in town.

LILIHA BAKERY AND COFFEE SHOP

515 N. Kuakini St. • 531-1651
from 6 a.m. Tuesday to 8 p.m. Sunday
BYOB? No • Credit cards? No
per person: $3-$6

One of the neat things about eating at this 55-year-old institution is that the only seating is at a long counter; from that vantage point you're right on top of the fry cooks at their griddles, and watching a good fry cook at work is one of the pleasures of casual eating. But first there's the ever-present line—"this place is rocking every day," says the young woman standing next to me in line—and she means even at three in the morning. But while you're waiting you do get to case the wildly decorated sheet cakes at the bakery counter, and might even pick up a couple of those well-known coco puffs: a deliciously sweet concoction of pastry filled with rich chocolate and topped with a deadly sweet chantilly sauce. Once you've got that coveted seat at the counter, in a room that probably hasn't changed much since they opened, and while sipping a cup of private brand roast coffee, you might try the pancakes. But then you have to remember that the butter rolls that come as a side on some dishes are scrumptious too, and between bursts of laughter and banter with the waitress, you might want to consider country-style scrambled eggs, with green and Spanish onions, tomato, and a choice of meat (Vienna sausage, maybe?). Another selection is the deluxe hamburger, one of the best of the breed, with a homemade patty on homemade rolls, plus creamy relish, lettuce, tomato, and onion. How about a thick, cakelike wedge of sweet bread French toast, soggy and sticking to the roof of your mouth?

Bottom Line: A long-running, open-all-night institution, great for eggs, sandwiches, and pastries.

NEW UPTOWN FOUNTAIN

522 N. School St. • 537-1881
Monday–Saturday 6:15 a.m.-12:45 p.m., 5 p.m.-7:15 p.m.
Sunday 7 a.m.-12:45 p.m.
BYOB? No • Credit cards? No
per person: $3-$5

Don't think banana split, hot fudge sundae, or strawberry ice cream soda. The name on the storefront is a misnomer. That is, if you can even find the place, on School Street just off the *mauka* corner of Liliha. I drove past twice the first time before I finally spotted it, in a two-story commercial building next to a lei shop behind the several cars that usually fill the minuscule parking lot. Once inside, you might find a handful of unfamiliar names on the menu. That's because when Tom and Shirley Higa took over the long-running business from an uncle in 1983, they added a few Okinawan touches. That was lucky for us, since a couple of these dishes are outstanding. Take the *warabaa*. It's like a loco moco, just as large, with three eggs fixed any way you wish, over scoops of rice, but topped with sweet pickles and doused with a choice of curry or stew sauce, all of it richly soaking into the rice. *'Ono!* Or *tachi*, two small hamburger steak patties made with their own hamburger mix (which includes lots of onion), cooked crisp on the outside and left moist inside, best served between soft buns with a touch of mayonnaise. The room itself is pretty patched up, with peeling walls and Formica tables, and maybe a box or two of yellow ripe papayas on the counter, the walls covered with classic older food signs—real collectibles—and dozens of descriptive menu signs that probably haven't been changed in years except for the prices. Variety is everywhere, in dishes ranging from bentos to bacon, lettuce, and tomato sandwiches; *saimin* to liver and onions; roast chicken to oatmeal.

Bottom Line: Put a hint of Okinawa together with a constant stream of neighborhood customers, add at least one beautifully *'ono* dish, and you've got proven staying power.

Kapiolani Coffee Shop (Kam Bowl)

1520 N. School St. • 845-3687
daily 7 a.m.-11 p.m.
BYOB? No • Credit cards? No
per person: $3-$7

If you're a bowler you may already be hanging out here. Same goes if you dig oxtail or pig's feet soup, or if you just enjoy the roar of all those lanes in action, with sudden bursts of congratulatory whoops when there's a strike. Don't wait for it to quiet down; the place rocks and bowls from early to late, and back to your left as you walk in the coffee shop is wide open to all the action. A couple of regulars are usually hunched over coffee at the counter, perhaps munching on a bacon and egg sandwich between frames, while others relax at a table. Breakfast is a busy time, let's say from seven to nine, but the 12 to 2 lunch crowd pretty much fills the seating, even if it does turn over fast. Fast? The service is amazingly quick and professional, and the food much better than you'd expect in a bowling alley, which may be why owner Gary Mijo, who's been here since 1986, has opened another, similar shop in Waimalu. The menu is simple. One good choice is kim chee fried rice with eggs on top, crunchy with cabbage and green onions. Mijo's oxtail soup is in a tie, he says, for popularity with the pig's feet soup: we're obviously in a down-home market. The oxtail broth is especially tasty, laced with green onions, Chinese parsley and even peanuts, with maybe a touch of *shoyu* or chile water stirred in to taste. The pig's feet bowl includes watercress, squash, and *limu*. Popular daily specials are corned beef and cabbage, beef tongue and short ribs— surprisingly, they're not *kal bi*, but thick-cut, in a Spanish sauce.

Bottom Line: Good, simple local food enjoyed in the roar of the adjoining lanes.

MITSU-KEN OKAZU AND CATERING

1223 N. School Street • 848-5573
Monday–Friday 4:30 a.m.-1 p.m., Saturday 4:30 a.m.-12 p.m.
BYOB? No • Credit cards? No
per person: $3-$5

There's nearly always a line out the door of Mitsu-Ken, one of the best-known *okazuya* on the island. The place is as tiny as tiny can get, so small there's room for maybe three very friendly adults inside at one time—which may be one reason for that ever-present line outside. Garlic chicken is another reason. Partners Brad Kaneshiro and Lyle Nonaka, in that shabby couple of blocks of School Street in Pālama that boast several of Honolulu's most mouth-watering *okazuya*, have been dishing out their good food for eleven years now, doing tons of takeout business, but also providing a couple of faded purple tables in front for those of us who can't wait until we get home. Their garlic chicken—whose fame extends well beyond the neighborhood—is crisp and tender, cooked just right, so flavorful you can smell it coming. Several other especially *'ono* dishes include *inari* sushi and *maki* sushi, and a melt-in-your-mouth *sari sari*, crowded with succulent pork, eggplant, and green beans. Pork tofu and hefty slabs of vegetable tempura are appealing additions to a plate, and talk about value: a breakfast special for less than two dollars includes fried rice, bacon, and eggs. Bentos can be made to order, but the most popular model comes with garlic chicken, egg omelet, hot dog, teri beef, Spam, and rice. The food's so tempting, and so much of it goes out that door all day long, you know the the kitchen in the back just MUST be a lot bigger than the front area.

Bottom Line: Some of the best *okazuya* dishes around.

YUKI'S

1320 N. School St. • 842-6046
Monday–Saturday 8 a.m.-midafternoon
BYOB? No • Credit cards? No
per person: $2-$6

Hard to tell just what Yuki's originally intended to be. In the telephone book it says Coffee House. Inside the ramshackle building it says Restaurant and on the battered sign on the street outside, just a few blocks from the Bishop Museum in Pālama, it says bento and *okazu*. Whatever it is it's good, really good. The place is beat up, inside and out, holes in the screens, concrete brick walls, linoleum floors, and stacks of cardboard boxes. But the food, to those who eat in—they do a tremendous takeout business—is served on real plates, not plastic, with real silverware. The menu is one of the most interesting in town. There is a simply delicious mahimahi stuffed with crab, imitation crab, and vegetables, baked and layered with a cream sauce; beautiful crispy fried chicken; tender chicken marinated in *shoyu* and stuffed with *gobo*, spinach roll stuffed with crab and fish (get there early for this one), fresh and thick and excellent *maki* sushi. Lunchtime can be mobbed, so maybe the best time to drop in is just after the rush; grab a seat at one of four tables and munch away. This is not the sort of place you think about for dessert, but you know what? Yuki's puts out a pretty decent sweet potato pie, sort of a turnover.

Bottom Line: Unless someone from the neighborhood has given him a steer, you're not about to bump into a wandering tourist here, so we get all this good stuff for ourselves.

La Mariana Sailing Club, Inc.

50 Sand Island Access Rd. • 848-2800
Monday 11 a.m.-8 p.m., Tuesday–Thursday 11 a.m.-9 p.m.
Friday 11 a.m.-11:30 p.m., Saturday–Sunday 11 a.m.-9 p.m.
BYOB? No, full bar • Credit cards? Yes
per person: $11-$22

Don't, please don't, come for the food. But if you want South Pacific kitsch and an offbeat location, this throwback to the 50s is about as thrown back as you can get. Lots of "tropical" here, on the docks at Ke'ehi Lagoon down a lane off the main Sand Island drag, where liveaboards straggle off their boats to the bar, conversations compete with the roar of jets taking off from the nearby airport, and, on most nights, there's live music from the piano, sometimes accompanied by a ukulele. Although there's a handful of tables on an outside deck, inside high-backed rattan chairs nestle among old fishnets, wall aquariums, and colored lights strung from the ceiling. Annette Nahinu, whose voluminous literature on each table regales visitors with her struggles to survive at the location since the mid-fifties, is quite a character—in keeping with her menu. If you must eat, then *lumpia* might be the best selection on the appetizer list, dipped in a sauce of vinegar, garlic, and chile peppers. The mahimahi sandwich holds its own, and among entrées mahimahi florentine isn't so bad. Stuffed eggplant *au gratin* gets its own shot at character with a crisply breaded outside, crammed inside with scallops, fish, and shrimp. And though a place like this couldn't do without its prime rib, the most interesting piece of red meat actually is garlic steak with anchovies. The character here isn't in the food, it's in the nostalgia. That's why we've come.

Bottom Line: Shades of the 1950s in an atmosphere-crammed place on the water where it's the feeling, not the food.

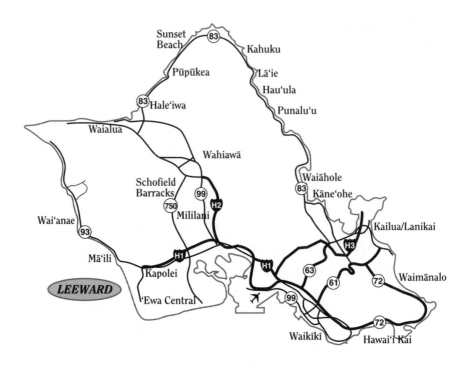

LEEWARD

ʻEwa Central
Moshi Moshi Tei

Kapolei
Julie'z Restaurant

Māʻili
Aunty's Seaside Cafe

Waiʻanae
Aloha Aina Cafe
Hannara Restaurant

MOSHI MOSHI TEI

91-1401 Fort Weaver Rd. • 685-2800
Tuesday–Sunday 11:30 a.m.-2:30 p.m., 5 p.m.-9 p.m.
BYOB? No, beer and wine served • Credit cards? Yes
per person: $6-$16

When Hawaiʻi goes to the suburbs these days, it brings its restaurants with it. Moshi Moshi is a good example of that slice of island dining found in the shopping malls of western Oʻahu, restaurants that have sprung up to serve commuters, soccer moms, and Little League dads. They're neutral dining havens, seeming somehow to lack that certain slice of character, in both decor and menu, that we enjoy so much in older, more established communities. What owner Kumiko Iseki has done is to bring a slice of Anglicized Japan to the Hawaiʻi suburbs at her location in front of ʻEwa Town Center, fitting perfectly into her market. The open, wood-trimmed dining room is well though subtly lit, seating perhaps eighty diners, and the place is sometimes so kid-friendly that, unless the kids are your own—maybe even if they are your own—you'll ask for a table on the other side of the room. The menu runs the spectrum of conventional Japanese cuisine, doing a decent job with those items its patrons like best. That simplest of sushi, the *inari*, gets flying colors, as does a good-as-downtown *unagi* and avocado roll. Maybe they do serve a lot of it, but me, I'd find something else to order besides the tempura, most charitably described as uninspired. Move on to a succulent slab of *misoyaki* butterfish with a squeeze of lemon, or *oyako don,* a bowl with enough food for two at least—heavy with chicken, green onions, Spanish onions, egg, and rice. That startlingly gorgeous dish you just saw go by on its way to someone else's table? Spicy calamari salad.

Bottom Line: Conventional Japanese food in a conventional suburban location.

JULIE'Z RESTAURANT

590 Farrington Hwy. • 693-8778
Sunday–Thursday 6 a.m.-9 p.m., Friday–Saturday 6 a.m.-11 p.m.
BYOB? Yes • Credit cards? Yes
per person: $5-$7

If you're one of those Hawaiian foodies who insist you find "authentic" Filipino food only in grubby old restaurants buried away in downtown Honolulu or on a back street in Waipahu, this may not be for you. Julie Oasay and Zenaida Pagdilao—who do the cooking—and their partner Ralph Fukushima (how'd he get in here, anyway?) have gone modern. They've opened with a contemporary look at the *makai* end of the Marketplace at Kapolei, where many of the suburb's restaurants are grouped. The look inside is large and light, with high black stools at the counter and tables in dark greens and blacks. At one side is an all-you-can-eat buffet with most—but not all—of the dishes featured on the menu. Simple stuff—like the ever-present *pancit* or pork adobo omelet—is just okay; a selected few traditional plates are much better, even though it's got to be said that the cuisine is cautious with its spices. Could that be because of the nature of diners in Kapolei's middle-class suburban market? Have we run into a "comfort zone" in Filipino food? Still, the pork *sari sari*, which includes squash and baby shrimp, is a warm, comforting dish, and Shanghai *lumpia* is exceptionally crisp, deliciously filled with pork hash. *Gisantes* hold their own on the bill of fare, but for a table of aficionados who really want to get into it, *dinuguan* is a favorite choice, the pork simmered to tenderness in its sauce of thickened blood. Not feeling that adventurous? Turn to the sandwiches and local lunch plates.

Bottom Line: Clean-cut Filipino food, gently spiced for the neighborhood palate.

Aunty's Seaside Cafe

87-730 Farrington Hwy. • 668-5177
daily 7 a.m.-3 p.m.
BYOB? No • Credit cards? Yes
per person: $3-$7

Carol Aiwohi's husband Richard is a construction worker. In 1995, when Carol opened her small, pink-trimmed restaurant set back from the highway under a banyan tree just ʻEwa of Waiʻanae, Richard got into the habit of grilling himself a sandwich before he went to work early in the morning. The sandwich—grilled Portuguese sweet bread lathered with cheese and slices of Portuguese sausage, very soft and mouth-filling—became a favorite menu item. The rest of the bill of fare in the wooden-ceilinged, 32-seat space covers the spectrum from hamburgers through sandwiches, plate lunches and noodle dishes. If you're not eating inside, or taking home, it's very nice to walk across the highway to the picnic tables on the lawn at Māʻili Beach. Another dish that's become very big with the citizens over the years, even if it is a bit greasy, is Richard's *lup cheong* fried rice, loaded with sausage. If corned beef hash is your thing for breakfast, you've got a choice. If you don't ask, Carol's sister Ericka, who most mornings is waiting tables, brings the canned variety (which isn't so bad, if you ask me). But if you inquire, there's a homemade version. The Seaside club sandwich is also a menu star, this one made of crab salad, ham, bacon, avocado, and tomato. And the garlic chicken on fried noodles—tasty noodles topped with tender chunks of deep-fried chicken—is a fine dish, loaded with textures.

Bottom Line: Easy-to-miss small restaurant with a handful of appetizing selections.

ALOHA AINA CAFE

85-773 Farrington Highway • 697-8808
Monday–Saturday 6 a.m.-4 p.m.
BYOB? No • Credit cards? No
per person: $4-$6

The little cafe is new, and most of us know that the odds aren't good for the success of a small restaurant. It's one of the toughest of all small businesses, and this one, run by a co-operative, is in a difficult area. I hope they stay around, because the food is darned good, even though I was put off at first: it's a "sprouty" place, with a bill of fare featuring veggie salads, organic lemonade, and taro burgers. But when you sit down at a table on the covered porch of the gray wooden house, set back from the highway in the same block as the KFC store, and they start bringing the food, things get good. I bit into the taro burger. Delicious! A crunchy, crispy taro patty on a fresh doughy bun surrounded by lettuce and sprouts, a good savory sauce, tomato, and a slice of cheese. It turns out that the co-op, called Ma'o, under the auspices of the Wai'anae Community Redevelopment Corporation, grows a lot of its own produce up in a nearby valley. The bean soup is misnamed. It is really a stew, one of the best stews around, rich and full of perfectly seasoned beans, rice, carrots, ham hocks, sausage, and potatoes. And there's a *kālua* quesadilla, a layer of pig cooked with jack cheese in a flour tortilla. Very, very tasty. Breakfast is banana pancakes and French toast made with either taro bread or Hawaiian sweet bread, or you might order a chili and rice omelet.

Bottom Line: Unexpectedly good food even if it is on a "healthy" menu.

Hannara Restaurant

86-078 Farrington Highway • 696-6137
Monday–Saturday 6 a.m.-8 p.m., Sunday 6 a.m.-3 p.m.
BYOB? Yes • Credit cards? No
per person: $3-$8

ISLAND OF OʻAHU • LEEWARD • WAIʻANAE

There's not really much in the way of restaurant eating—let alone "dining"—out on the west end of Oʻahu. Hannara is one of only a handful of actual sit-down restaurants in the Waiʻanae-Nānākuli area, hidden behind the parking off the highway Waiʻanae of the Longs Drugstore. The dining room is large and open with a counter on one side, tables and booths filling the rest. Even if the name is Japanese, very little on the menu is: Sandwiches, American Food, Hawaiian Food, and Korean Food. So what's really to eat here? A lovely ponytailed waitress will tell you that breakfast is okay, but a glance at the bill of fare shows nothing out of the ordinary. It's not until lunch that we get into the nitty gritty of the place. A sign on the wall behind the counter says their hamburger steak is the "best on the Leeward coast." Not much of an honor perhaps, but you know what? They're right. Good meat, floating in a thin gravy and covered with onions. Not much to look at, but the *ʻono* seasonings make it worthy of the boast. You can try the Hawaiian Plate or the Hannara Special, but it's better to just select à la carte. Best in the Korean category are *kal bi,* meat *jun,* and fried *man doo.* Forget the seafood, which is frequently overcooked. From the Hawaiian plate select a flavorful pork *laulau* and maybe some *kālua* pig. One day as I was leaving, I said to Charlie Han, who with wife Christina has owned the restaurant since 1988, "Really small"— referring to the price of the $1.50 hamburger. All Charlie did was smile.

Bottom Line: An actual restaurant serving decent food in an area where restaurants are scarce.

ISLAND OF
HAWAI'I

Captain Cook
Manago Hotel

Hilo
Hilo Rice Noodle Soup
Ken's House of Pancakes

Honalo
Teshima's Restaurant

Kona
Charley's Thai Cuisine
Kona Mix Plate
Ocean View Inn
Paul Muranaka's

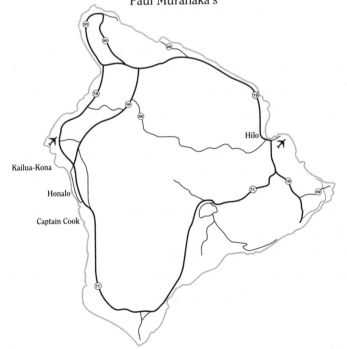

MANAGO HOTEL

82-6155 Māmalahoa Hwy. • 323-2642
Tuesday–Sunday 7 a.m.-9 a.m. (breakfast),
11 a.m.-2 p.m. (lunch), 5 p.m.-7:30 p.m. (dinner)
BYOB? No, a full service bar • Credit cards? Yes
per person: $7-$10

High ceilings, slowly rotating fans, well-worn wooden floors, widely spaced tables, and, on the wall, the menu: liver and onions, pork chops, steak, hamburger. Sounds like a cafeteria or boarding house in the Midwest—except that through the window are coconut palms and the ocean. And the location is Captain Cook, Hawai'i, which means the food might not be what it appears to be on the menu. Let's call this middle America with coconuts. The little side dishes brought almost immediately to the tables are cold black-eyed peas doused with sugar, outstanding potato salad flavored with bits of tuna, exceptionally tasty vegetables, and, if you're lucky, a small dish they'd never understand in a Midwest cafeteria—pickled *limu* with onions and tomatoes. At Manago, where Dwight Manago is the third generation to be running the old wooden-framed hotel and restaurant on the highway, the sides may be the best thing. All too often the meat comes overcooked (there's that Midwestern touch for you), although it's hard not to agree that the pork chops that overflow their platter are among the best on the island, and the seasonings on everything are great. There's a reason for that flavor, a secret, but one that's not difficult to pry out of the waitress: it's the pan, a large, rectangular fifty-year-old cast iron pan that, with salt and pepper and cottonseed oil, is all they use to flavor the meat and fish dishes, even a house specialty such as *'ōpelu*, fresh out of the channel and best eaten dipped in chile water with a dash of *shoyu*.

Bottom Line: A unique, long-running institution where Hawai'i's flavors tweak down-home American cuisine.

HILO RICE NOODLE SOUP

1990 Kino'ole St., • 981-5841
Monday–Saturday 9:30 a.m.-8 p.m.
BYOB? Yes • Credit cards? Yes
per person: $5-$8

Try this scenario: you're a passenger on a cruise ship tied up for the day at the dock in Hilo Bay while its passengers take in the town's attractions. You've worked up a romance with a fellow passenger and arranged to meet onshore where, sophisticated guy that you are, you'll feed the damsel with real "local color." Someplace, of course, where there's absolutely no chance of running into another passenger. Who needs the gossip? Let me tell you, Hilo Rice Noodle, almost the only store left open in Kino'ole Shopping Center in south Hilo next to the big space that used to be the Food Fair market, is as much color as you could ask for—and the food is worth the effort. You, savvy lover that you are, know to ignore the long list of *phô* dishes. Never mind that fellow diners are slurping it up, it's no better than a mediocre broth. What you want is chicken garlic, a dish you'll smell coming twenty feet away, rich with mushrooms, perfectly cooked chicken and ginger, served on a platter of rice. Match this with salt and pepper squid, hot and crisp and chewy, beautifully prepared with its own hints of garlic. And, to mellow it all down, a plate of salted fish-fried rice, filled with egg, cabbage, and green onions. It may not be bursting with romance, but the red plastic tables at which you eat on the patio and the smiling waitress who speaks thirty-seven words of English are real Hilo. Never mind that since Food Fair is gone you've go to remember to stop someplace else to pick up the beer.

Bottom Line: Excellent eating in a Hilo neighborhood—but forget about the name of the restaurant when you order.

KEN'S HOUSE OF PANCAKES

1730 Kamehameha Ave. • 935-8711
open 24 hours
BYOB? No • Credit cards? Yes
per person: $5-$9

Looking for someplace everyone hasn't already discovered, a hidden place with modest menu and no reputation at all? Look someplace else, Ken's is none of the above. There's not a soul in town who couldn't tell you exactly where Ken's is—and probably most of the menu choices. Need directions? "Go down to Ken's and turn right." For over 30 years, if you've wanted buttermilk pancakes, or any of more than seventy other menus items (count 'em, they're numbered), from fried chicken to spaghetti, this is where Hilo's hungry citizens have come, especially for the pancakes, sweet bread French toast, and waffles, all hugely popular at the intersection of Highways 19 and 11. If there's any doubt, all you've got to do is look for the only place around with a line in front, even though inside they've got two large dining rooms plus a counter, all of it going twenty-four hours a day. The waitresses in short, flowered Hawaiian dresses are pros, crowding tables with guava, coconut, maple, and *likoʻi* syrups, extra butter, and coffee refills. But that lengthy menu is more than pancakes, lots more. Take "Da Bradah"; now there's an omelet, bursting with bacon, ham and Portuguese sausage, plus green onions and cheese. Well, maybe it could use a touch of Tabasco sauce. And Ken's corned beef hash isn't your usual—mostly potato—Hawaiian variety. This one is mostly corned beef, very tasty, especially when it's buried in a corned beef hash *moco*. They'll bring your bacon extra crisp if you ask.

Bottom Line: Big reputation, big menu, big spot.

TESHIMA'S RESTAURANT

79-7251 Māmalahoa Highway • 322-9140
daily 6:30 a.m.-1:45 p.m., 5 p.m.-9 p.m.
BYOB? No, full bar • Credit cards? No
per person: $8-$12

Mama's come a long way since she started selling sandwiches during the war. Ninety-seven years old and a legend on her part of the coast, she's still hands-on, still working the room. "This is my life," says Shizuko Teshima, of a life that's built one of the most popular restaurants on the Kona coast. Often there's a brief wait for a space in the crowded parking lot, but inside there's plenty of seating in several large rooms separated by tatami screens, the tables filled with locals and affluent *haoles* who live nearby. Mama's waitresses are Hawai'i's classics, leaning over your table with a flower behind one ear, clad in anything from *holukū* to tight, short skirts, making suggestions, bringing another drink from the bar—which serves short drinks with a good pour. Meals begin with a complimentary appetizer of *maki* sushi. What regulars order most often is *teishoku,* usually the one with miso soup, sashimi, sukiyaki, shrimp or vegetable tempura, *sunomono,* and *tsukemono.* The tempura is luscious and the sukiyaki, although a modest-sized bowl, exceptionally appetizing. Island butterfish, which comes either teriyaki style—the sauce nearly stew-like and with delicious tofu—or breaded in *panko,* is a stand-out, and so is the Kona fried rice platter, which, although it's got its share of oil, is addictive with its carrots, onions, and, at your choice, chicken. Oh, remember those sandwiches that got Mama started during the war? They're still on the menu, even if their prices may have changed a bit.

Bottom Line: Good food, lots of history in a fun restaurant on the highway.

117

CHARLEY'S THAI CUISINE

74-5586 Palani Rd. • 334-0891
Monday–Saturday 10 a.m.-9 p.m., Sunday 11 a.m.-9 p.m.
BYOB? Yes • Credit cards? Yes
per person: $6-$9

"Family run," at least in Hawai'i, nearly always means a welcoming, cordial room and usually good homestyle food. Our islands belie cynical comments like, "If I want Mom's cooking, I'll eat at home," or writer Nelson Algren's, "Never play cards with a man called Doc. Never eat at a place called Mom's." Which brings us to Charley's, hidden way inside the Kona Coast Shopping Center above downtown, where Mom, Mantha Chaleunvong, is usually in the kitchen (Charley cooks in their newer restaurant up in Waimea). Mantha's dishes are hot, fresh, and crisp. Too bad that occasionally a server in the twenty-two-seat, blue-tinted room with tables outside is slow and unresponsive to customers. Try to ignore all that, because Mom's dishes are what we're here for. Begin with sharing one of the better green papaya salads, the papaya shredded with tomatoes and green beans and laced with ground peanuts and lemon juice, best ordered medium spicy. Yum. Then, since portions are large, another couple of plates to share, even if *phad thai* would be enough by itself, enhanced by adding, chicken, beef, pork, or mahimahi. One of Charley's particular house specials, the popular garlic shrimp sautéed with curried coconut sauce, is especially tasty, the chunks of crisp, fresh cucumbers and tomatoes going perfectly with the sauce. And afterwards, there's a delicious gelato place next door.

Bottom Line: You've got to find it, and service can be frustrating, but they've got some good food.

KONA MIX PLATE

75-5660; Kopiko St. • 329-8104
Monday–Saturday 10 a.m.-8 p.m.
BYOB? No • Credit cards? No
per person: $5-$11

It's not often you find a local plate lunch spot that's not open for breakfast. Maybe Mom liked to sleep in, because although it was she who originally started the business in a store across the street, her kids seem to be doing all right at the present site without that hearty Hawaiian morning meal. In Kopiko Plaza storefront, above downtown Kona and behind the Burger King, brothers Inbea and Ricky Kim's plain, light room, with linoleum floors and T-bar ceiling, does its busiest hours between about eleven and two, and a few hours later the dinner menu draws the neighborhood clientele in early. The rest of the day the stream of customers ebbs and flows. I must say I disagree with customer preference here: the *bulgogi* plate is obviously the restaurant's most popular meal, but I've found it drier than it should be, even if the *shoyu,* sugar, garlic, and green onion marinade does make its flavoring fine. Better: a cup of Portuguese bean soup with a fried mahimahi sandwich. The soup is mildly spicy, a savory mixture of beans, ham hocks, pasta, and vegetables, and the two-piece fish sandwich fried crisp and light— it can also be ordered sautéed—served on a bun with lettuce and thick slices of tomato and onion, tartar sauce the dressing of choice. On Fridays, two sizes of prime rib are on the menu, good meat served as rare as you like it, au jus, with a small, simple and very good tossed green salad. An interesting side dish is crab *shu mai.*

Bottom Line: Freshly cooked, well-prepared plates.

OCEAN VIEW INN

75-5683 Ali'i St. • 329-9998
breakfast, 6:30 a.m.-11 a.m.; lunch, 11 a.m.-2:45 p.m.
dinner, 5:15 p.m.-9:45 p.m.
BYOB? No, full bar • Credit cards? No
per person: $4-$9

On the left, as you enter the faded building with the long line of windows facing out across Ali'i Drive to Kailua Bay in downtown Kona, is a single small table. Nearly every morning an older man sits there, obviously a regular. He probably hasn't been coming in for quite as long as the Kam family has been running Ocean View—nearly seventy-five years now—but he's obviously no newcomer, so you'd figure he knows what to order: corned beef hash. I'd follow his lead, but it turns out that the portion on the plate in front of him isn't, as you'd anticipate in such a well-worn local place, homemade. And even though I'm among that multitude that thinks Hormel's Mary Kitchen canned hash ought to be a staple in every kitchen, still, I'm a bit nonplused. Not homemade? How dare they? From now on, I'll listen to the waitress—any waitress, since most of these women have been walking the battered orange and black linoleum-tiled floors for years and the menu is a huge one. The morning's recommendations are likely to be beef stew—a version of this dish that looks and tastes canned, although it isn't—or Portuguese sausage and eggs. Later in the day, you'll get a crack at a dish that's not on the menu, the Tyron Special, made from scratch from shrimp and vegetables over crisp or soft noodles with sweet pork mixed in, or a big house favorite, the Chinese Plate—an overflowing platter of *chow mein*, sweet-and-sour pork ribs, egg foo young, steamed pork, and crisp won ton. Plus, their Hawaiian dishes aren't bad, and the bar in the next room does turn out a mighty tasty Bloody Mary.

Bottom Line: Great location, menu choices from roast pork sandwiches to spaghetti, and a real Hawaiian feeling of welcome.

PAUL MURANAKA'S

74-5490 Kaiwi St. • 331-1509
Monday–Friday 5 a.m.-1 p.m.
BYOB? No • Credit cards? No
per person: $4-$8

For those of us who love eating, the dream is of finding our very own hole-in-the-wall—a hidden gourmet treasure, an oasis unknown to most of our acquaintances, unheralded in guidebooks and not so easy to find. A gem like Paul and Barbara Muranaka's, built into an industrial bay off Kaiwi Street behind Gray's Furniture in the old industrial area of Kona. Boy, what they've been doing with food in that store for the last six years! I first ate there one dark morning before sunrise, when we were guided to the door by the light of the "open" neon sign in the window. Inside was a small, clean space with half a dozen tables on a concrete floor. Up front was Barbara, a musician of note and hula instructor. Back in the kitchen, out of sight, was Paul, who, among other accomplishments, was once executive chef at a Sam Choy's restaurant. His breakfast might be the best in town: Oriental shrimp omelet crowded with green onions, fish cake, fresh shiitake mushrooms, onions, shrimp, and, for added flavor, bok choy; sweet bread French toast, dipped in eggs and—get this—orange juice, for a special tang; eggs scrambled perfectly, flecked with green onions—believe it or not, not everyone behind a grill does eggs well. And there's a croissant dish, mushy with cheese, eggs, and a choice of meats (Spam for me). At lunchtime one of the best dishes, which the police clientele regularly enjoys, is *pūlehu*—either beef or chicken—a fabulous dish, marinated in pepper, Hawaiian salt, oil and garlic, cooked on a griddle and doused with crisp garlic. Other favorites include Korean chicken and Paul's excellent loco moco, special because of his own brown gravy.

Bottom Line: Each dish is a fine one in this obscure corner of culinary heaven.

ISLAND OF
KAUA'I

Hanalei
Polynesia Cafe

Hanapēpē
Green Garden

Kalāheo
Camp House Grill
Kalaheo Steak House

Kapa'a
Ono Family Restaurant

Līhu'e
Lihue Barbecue Inn

Po'ipū
Puka Dog

Puhi
Mark's Place

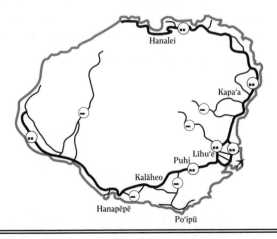

POLYNESIA CAFE

5-5190 Kūhiō Highway • 826-1999
daily 8 a.m.-9 p.m.
BYOB? Yes • Credit cards? Yes
per person: $7-$11

In this fascinating little spot, hidden behind another tiny restaurant in the Ching Young Center just off the highway in downtown Hanalei, the owners claim they dish out "gourmet food on paper plates." They're right, both about the food and the plates. Jhoane and Thames Goodwin (he hails from Texas and she's an Englishwoman), in their casual, open, breezy diner do have maybe the most interesting food operation on their end of the island. They make their own pastries—great muffins and wonderful mopecho (chocolate chip, pecan and macadamia nut) cookies. The French fries that come with the local organic meat hamburgers are maybe the best on the island—cooked in good, fresh oil, the skins left on—even if the hamburger itself can get a little dry because it's not very fatty. They're heavy on local seafood, like 'ahi tacos or grilled mahimahi plates, and they're working on developing a larger, locally accented Mexican menu. Meanwhile, the Hawaiian variety plate is loaded with fine *poke*, good *lomi* salmon, and tasty, smoky *kālua* pork. Breakfast ranges from waffles to *huevos rancheros*. "If we can make it ourselves," says Tim Goodwin, "I don't want to buy it," although they do get their tortillas from Sinaloa in Honolulu. Hey, this casual spot could actually become a real gourmet restaurant.

Bottom Line: An appetizing, eclectic menu in an easygoing location serving good food at value-wise prices.

GREEN GARDEN

1-3749 Kaumuali'i Hwy. • 335-5422
Wednesday–Monday 5 p.m.-9 p.m.
BYOB? No, full bar. • Credit cards? Yes
per person: $13-$21

Mom would have loved it: the coral-colored tablecloths and rattan chairs, potted plants and *mai tais*. Plus the special *liliko'i* daiquiris. And why not? Green Garden is a throwback to another era, to 1948, when Gwen Hamabata's (she's the boss these days) family began this open, multileveled restaurant now buried in a minijungle of tropical foliage at the triangle where the old original road curves back to meet the newer Highway 50. The restaurant's menu runs the spectrum, from *'ahi* A L'Arashiro—tuna in a dressing sauce of shiitake and button mushrooms, with onions and mayonnaise (a moist and flaky dish)—to a plate of pork chops that should have come off the *kiawe* broiler grill a little bit sooner. And even though the fried rice that comes as a choice with many of the dishes is unfortunately very much like the rice Mom used to make, it goes pretty well with shrimp tempura, or the popular East-West special: a small char-broiled teriyaki steak that shares a plate with deep-fried shrimp. Fresh fish are always big on the "Specials" board near the front door, although it's sometimes a good idea to ask the kitchen to undercook that fish. Sauces can be intriguing, like the Kaua'i pepper and pineapple sauce over grilled *ono*, a delicious mixture of sweet and spicy. And—Mom would have appreciated this—the small salad bar is really good.

Bottom Line: An attractive, generation-spanning spot in which to enjoy an interesting dish or two, particularly a saucy one.

CAMP HOUSE GRILL

2-2431 Kaumuali'i Hwy. • 332-9755
daily 6 a.m.-9 p.m.
BYOB? No, beer and wine available • Credit cards? Yes
per person: $4-$14

Inside the pale blue batten board building on the corner of Highway 50 and Papalina Road in Kalāheo the walls are white and the floors dark scarred plywood, all very much in keeping with the "camp house" theme from the area's old plantation days. Except I'd be surprised if the plantation workers got a look at this kind of menu. Big on breakfast, but also boasting an extensive list of hamburgers—mostly wolfed down by the lunch crowd—and dishes like grilled chicken, the catch of the day, or BBQ pork ribs. One of the waitresses swears by the hamburger that comes with grilled pineapple, teriyaki sauce, lettuce, tomato, Swiss cheese, and mayonnaise. Another goes for the patty with sautéed mushrooms, lettuce, tomato, Swiss cheese, and mayonnaise. Nearly everyone in the neighborhood agrees they're about the best hamburgers in town; maybe, they say, the best on the island. But the menu certainly does have some of the best breakfast fare in the islands. The sausage gravy and biscuits are a meal in themselves, a truly fine dish. That also comes with the Paniolo breakfast and its scrambled eggs on ham. The restaurant's loco moco isn't bad, although there's an extra charge to include onions and mushrooms in the gravy. Nearly everything, owner Nick Morrison (who has another House up in Kapa'a) says, is homemade, and although he doesn't claim to have brewed the local Keoki beer that they have on tap, he can claim credit for the pie list, headed by pineapple cream cheese and macadamia nut. Exceptionally good crusts.

Bottom Line: Good food, reasonable prices, and maybe the best biscuits and gravy in Hawai'i.

KALAHEO STEAK HOUSE

4444 Papalina Rd. • 332-9780
daily 6 p.m.-10 p.m.
BYOB? No, full bar • Credit cards? Yes
per person: $18-$24

Want your drink sweetened a bit? Just ask. That's the way they are inside the green ramshackle building that houses Randall Eneim's steak joint. Eneim, who comes out of a restaurant family on Maui, has owned the restaurant in Kalaheo, just off Highway 50, for the last dozen years. The customers sitting in the dimly lit room in captain's chairs are mostly Hawaiians and resident haoles, and there's the appetizing aroma of grilling meats and sizzling pans. Kids are obviously at home here, and service can be lax. The small bar is hidden at the back, where you're likely to miss it if you don't ask and you're not a regular. The meat is neither the cheap Select quality nor the pricier Prime. Instead they serve Choice cuts that can't be called great, but are still pretty good, and the steaks are not great, but still decent cuts, mostly top sirloins and New Yorks. Prime rib is a good choice and so are baby back ribs. This is a meat house, so perhaps the grilled fish dishes are best avoided. Appetizers and side dishes can sometimes actually be a better bet than entrées. Calamari steak appetizer is deep fried in a crusty *panko* batter and happily laced with capers and a lemon sauce. Salads are much better than you'd expect and so is the Portuguese bean soup. If they're serving the homemade *liliko'i* cheesecake, grab it.

Bottom Line: Decent meats with a good bar in a comfortable setting.

ONO FAMILY RESTAURANT

4-1292 Kūhiō Highway • 822-1710
daily 7 a.m.-2 p.m.
BYOB? No • Credit cards? Yes
per person: $5-$7

Breakfast is the name of the game here. Yeah, they're open for lunch, but just try and get a booth or a table right away on a Saturday or Sunday morning. "We've got a full house," the hostess will say, and probably has been saying since 1979. But it's a fairly large restaurant and the wait is seldom long. When you walk into the old frame building that used to be a movie theater on the side of the highway, you're back in the 1940s, plantation style, with pinks and greens and folding shutters. In the earlier morning guests are likely to notice an elderly gentleman hand-winding the old clock in the corner, and if it turns out that you're in the mood for a hamburger that early in the morning, before they begin serving lunch, you can have it if you don't care that it's fried instead of grilled. It is the omelet list that's most impressive. Like your omelet out of the ordinary? Try the Local Boy, with cheese, a too-mild Portuguese sausage, and kim chee. On the other side of the bill of fare is the Lindsey Special, well-prepared fried rice topped with two eggs and a choice of either Spam or Portuguese sausage. And you certainly can't leave without trying the house loco moco, a modest version, eggs over rice with the gravy on the side.

Bottom Line: Good breakfast in a nostalgic building on the side of the road.

LIHUE BARBEQUE INN

2982 Kress St. • 245-2932
Monday–Saturday 7:30 a.m.-10:30 a.m. (breakfast)
10:30 a.m.-1:30 p.m. (lunch), Monday–Thursday 5 p.m.-8:30 p.m.
(dinner), Friday–Saturday 4:30 p.m.-8:45 p.m. (dinner)
BYOB? No, full bar • Credit cards? Yes
per person: $9-$22

It boasts long years in the business and the large portions we in Hawai'i nearly always expect, and the food's good, some of it very good. The fourth generation of the Sasaki family is now running the restaurant that Hanayo and Masaichi Sasaki began in a smaller version in 1940 just before the war in what today is a light industrial area just off Rice Street. Most of the food is still homemade, and locals and visitors still throng into the nondescript room with fans hanging from the ceiling and a television set and small service bar back in the corner. They do make their own soups, though they're pretty generic, and *saimin* is refreshingly absent from the menu list, even though there's a Japanese accent here and there. Seared scallop salad on a bed of greens, dressed in *liliko'i* vinaigrette, is a popular dish, or baby back ribs in barbecue sauce, the tender meat falling off the bones. There's also a mile-high *'ahi* sandwich, smothered in tomatoes, with the crunch of deep-fried Japanese eggplant and fresh onions. Two small side dishes are especially tasty: *somen* salad in a dressing of *shoyu* and vinegar with a "secret" ingredient, and a tasty little cole slaw with pineapple. On the dinner menu you can order a New Zealand rack of lamb, rock salt-roasted prime rib, or mahimahi stuffed with cheese, crab, and vegetables. Want the fast-selling homemade pie? Better get there early in the day.

Bottom Line: A long-standing, off-the-beaten-track restaurant with a good variety of solid, flavorful dishes.

PUKA DOG

2360 Kiahuna Plantation Dr. • 635-6354
Monday–Saturday 11 a.m.-6 p.m.
BYOB? Yes • Credit cards? Yes
per person: $6-$8

Hawai'i has this lovely habit of taking many of the foods and dishes that it imports and tweaking them, just a little, so that even if a dish arrives as a national classic—like the hot dog—it's got a chance of acquiring its own local identity. That's what's happened in the quiet, upscale Poipu Shopping Village, where Rick and Dominique Quinette, in their small, zephyr-cooled hot dog store with green rattan tables and chairs, serve the most mouth-watering sausage and bun combination you can imagine. They take this large, long, crusty roll, developed from a French bread recipe of a friend of Dominique's, and skewer it down onto a "toaster spike," which crisps up the inside and leaves the outside of the roll soft and mushy. The server then reaches over to the grill, lifts off a large (quarter pound), beautifully flavored hot dog (your choice of Polish or veggie), charred just a little, and slides it into that toasted hole in the roll, with a dash of your choice of mustard and a garlic-lemon sauce available in original, spicy, or hot versions. And— here's the big seller at this hot dog stand—a choice of homemade local relishes: papaya, coconut, banana, pineapple, mango, or star-fruit. Mango is the favorite, although Rick himself prefers the coconut. The charred sausage just by itself, in the stick-to-the-roof-of-your-mouth bun, would be fine. Add the other tastes and you end up rolling your tongue around the inside of your mouth to catch the flavors. The only other item on the menu: a home-squeezed lemonade, which may be a tad too sweet.

Bottom Line: A Hawai'i twist to an American classic brings out one of the best dishes in the islands.

MARK'S PLACE

610 Haleukana St. • 245-2522
Monday–Friday 10 a.m.-7 p.m.
BYOB? Yes • Credit cards? No
per person: $4-$6

You're not going to find this place by accident—unless your idea of sightseeing is cruising industrial parks. When you hit the main entrance to Kaua'i Community College on Highway 50 at Puhi turn *makai* on Puhi Road, then right on Hanalima to the corner of Haleukana. You might notice a fading cloth sign hanging from the roof on the corner building, or you might not. Mark Oyama, who five years ago began this clean, somewhat upscale plate lunch and bento store with a touch of sophistication, also teaches culinary classes at the school. Lunch at Mark's is some of the best local food on the island. Whether you're just walking across the small parking lot to eat at a picnic table outside under the *tacoma* trees with the roosters and flies, heading for the nearest park, the mountains, or down to the beach, when you walk out Mark's door your bag of goodies is likely to be full and heavy. The large bento is crammed with hash, Spam, macaroni salad, rice, teriyaki beef, chicken *katsu*, and *tsukemono*. The very popular combination plate almost needs two hands to carry, filled with succulent beef stew, fried noodles, chicken *katsu,* teriyaki beef, and—natch—macaroni salad. The mahimahi sandwich is big and soft, with lots of mayonnaise, and comes with especially good onion rings. Grilled, crusted salmon salad, frequently a special on the board, is a refreshingly light touch. Oh, might not want to forget dessert, like a two-layered chocolate mousse drizzled with raspberry sauce.

Bottom Line: Nicely priced, clean-cut local food with a bit of sophistication.

ISLAND OF MAUI

Hāna
Tutu's Snack Shop

Kahului
TJ's Oriental Food Mart & Fast Food

Kīhei
Da' Kitchen

Lahaina
Aloha Mixed Plate
Lahaina Sushila
Thai Chef

Makawao
Kitada's Kau Kau Corner

Wailuku
Sam Sato's Inc.

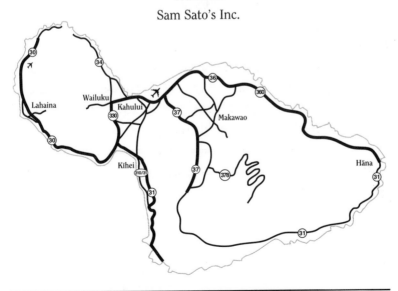

TUTU'S SNACK SHOP

Hāna Bay • 248-8224
daily 8 a.m.-4 p.m.
BYOB? Yes • Credit cards? No
per person: $5-$8

Two sorts of patrons—maybe three—line up at the window at Tutu's on Hāna Bay after driving the famed road to Hāna. First, those of us who neglected to pack a picnic lunch from a deli or *okazuya* before we hit the road. Second, those who've elected not to join the hordes up on the hill at the better known Hana Ranch Restaurant. And third, those of us who had always intended to stand in line, take our order, and walk across the street to tables scattered by the beach and enjoy the deep blue view across the small bay. True, the cheery service from the serving window at the small eatery in the community center building across from the Hana Canoe Club hut does provide several tables, but they'd blow away in a good breeze and besides, who'd eat there when you can dine within feet of the water? At the beach tables, though, you might be distracted, because at the next table you're likely to have visitors who've arrived in tour vans, bringing white linen, real wine glasses, and catered gourmet lunches. You, if you're a Tutu's customer, you'll be eating off plastic, and your choices will be a handful of plate lunches—the roast pork and gravy isn't bad—or sandwiches. On the sandwich list is a thick taro burger, smothered in fresh onions, tomatoes, and lettuce, or a chili dog, itself lathered with a mild meaty chile and beans, plus the usual hamburgers and BLTs, with breakfast served until eleven.

Bottom Line: The view's the thing, and besides, it's close to being the only game in town.

TJ's Oriental Food Mart & Fast Food

65 W. Ka'ahumanu Ave. • 893-0090
daily 7 a.m.-8 p.m.
BYOB? No, beer available in market • Credit cards? Yes
per person: $5-$6

Theirs is not the large supermarket out in front. It's in the back, and if someone hadn't told you, you'd never know John and Josie Jacaine were selling fish, vegetables, groceries, and hot food in their market at the rear of the mall, behind Ah Fook's Supermarket. Even when you go in you'll probably have to look around before spotting the hot food counter and oilcloth-covered tables in the right rear corner of the market. And you have to watch the timing: TJ's is one of those local food places where, no matter what the printed hours are, if you're there when they open you won't get much more than coffee, and in the couple of hours before closing the selection is limited. Between times, it's classic Filipino all the way. Each plate comes with a choice of rice or long rice, the latter far and away the best choice; two scoops white rice is everywhere, but long rice with vegetables, pork, and shrimp isn't. The *pinapaitan*, loaded with tripe, is hot and rich—some might say greasy—and helpings of *dnardaaraan* are savory and filling, but perhaps the best dish coming out of the kitchen is *pinacbet*, heavy in texture and flavor and luscious on the tongue. Your wandering visitor who's straggled off a visiting cruise ship isn't likely to find the place, so the clientele is purely Kahului and Wailuku, filling the tables at lunchtime and making a thin, steady stream the rest of the day.

Bottom Line: Interesting, inexpensive Filipino eating in a hard-to-find location.

DA' KITCHEN

2439 S. Kīhei Rd. • 875-7782
daily 9 a.m.-9 p.m.
BYOB? Yes • Credit cards? Yes
per person: $6-$8

ISLAND OF MAUI • KĪHEI

More rice, more fish, more quality. The kitchen's plate lunches are as large and heavy as they get, so don't let the prices—higher than most of the competition—scare you. It's worth it, because the owners (who absolutely hate to have anyone know their names) serve up one of the finest plate lunches on Maui, one that can hold its head up with—maybe even above—any plate lunch in Hawai'i. Set back toward the end of the Rainbow Mall next to a liquor store (that's where you go for the beer), they've developed a real following in the five years since starting the place; now they're running a second one over in Kahului, although that's a little more upscale, with waitresses, yet. The fish tempura plate is loaded with four fillets fried in clean oil in a light, herbed crust, truly an 'ono dish. The loco moco should be winning prizes—probably the heaviest plate in the house—with thick hamburger patties, a couple of eggs, and lots of onions sautéed with mushrooms in gravy covering the whole thing. The big *saimin* bowl is so loaded there's barely room for the broth, packed with beef teriyaki, fish cake, noodles, vegetables, and *char siu*. A rightfully popular dish is the Hawaiian plate, with a tiny helping of *lomi* salmon, large portion of *kālua* pork, succulent *laulau*, and some so-so long rice. Decor comes in clean-cut contemporary form, with blue back-lighting on wooden wall carvings spilling out over a clientele of locals, part-time condominium residents, and itinerant surfers.

Bottom Line: Killer plate lunches that come in large portions and well-cooked flavors.

ALOHA MIXED PLATE

1285 Front St. • 661-3322
daily 10:30 a.m.-10 p.m.
BYOB? No, full bar • Credit cards? Yes
per person: $4-$9

So, you want plate lunch—but with a touch of romance. Maybe a comfortable seat at a table beneath a large, shady *milo* tree and big green umbrellas. If it was right on the beach that would be all right, and while we're at it let's have a view across the Lahaina Roads to Moloka'i and Lāna'i. As a final touch, we'll add real live table service. That's the story at Aloha, on the Ka'anapali edge of Lahaina next to Old Lahaina Luau. It's an absolutely lovely setting, but that doesn't necessarily mean the food's any better—or even as good—as you'd find in maybe fifty other plate lunches in the islands. In spite of the multitude of "Best Plate Lunch" and "Best Appetizer" awards the menu claims, ordering gets tricky. To begin with, the rice is gummy, the macaroni salad completely undistinguished. The vaunted coconut prawns, served with chutney sauce, can be lumpy and strangely unsatisfying. On the other hand, where else outside a Chinese restaurant can you get a fine helping of Chinese roast duck on your plate lunch, even if the house does insist that their most popular plate is the Hawaiian platter with *kālua* pork, cabbage, *lomi* salmon, poi, macaroni salad, and rice. And if you're here anyway, but don't happen to be in a plate lunch mood, the noodle dishes, like *chow fun* or *look fun* in black bean garlic sauce, are deliciously appetizing. The mahimahi sandwich, with French fries and coleslaw (also undistinguished, what is it with these simple sides?), is fresh and perfectly cooked.

Bottom Line: Lots of variation in quality, but the plate lunches are served in a glorious setting.

LAHAINA SUSHILA

117 Prison St. • 661-5679
Monday–Saturday 6 a.m.-4 p.m.
BYOB? No • Credit cards? No
per person: $3-$6

It seems a bit incongruous when you think about it: this classic *okazuya* that's changed so little in nearly forty years finding itself today just three doors from Front Street and the horde of visitors with the latest beach fashions, SUVs, and cell phones. But the faded yellow building, run now by the daughter of the woman who opened its doors in 1965, is the real thing. The three battered, Formica-covered picnic tables inside are graced with fresh flowers, and in the early hours of the day trays of food are piled high behind the serving counter. But beware: although the posted hours say they're open until four in the afternoon, by about two the food choices have dwindled, and the best stuff is usually gone before noon. Great selection; makes you wonder how early they must've gotten up in the morning to have done it all by six. String beans and chicken, *maki* sushi and *inari* sushi, big helpings of beef stew and small cakes of corned beef hash that are crispy on the outside and almost chewy inside, fried fish and hamburger. *Shoyu* chicken is one of the most popular dishes, served in big pieces, just like the heavily breaded fried chicken. There's nothing small about any of the food behind that counter: even the deep-fried shrimp are larger than you'd expect at these prices, and unexpectedly good-tasting. If I were heading out of Lahaina to the beach or to the mountains, the road to Hāna or the airport—even to work—this is where I'd stop first.

Bottom Line: Fine example of a traditional *okazuya*, featuring a wide choice of appetizing, stick-to-the-ribs dishes.

THAI CHEF

880 Front St. • 667-2814
Monday–Friday 11 a.m.-2 p.m., daily 5 p.m. on
BYOB? Yes (even encouraged) • Credit cards? Yes
per person: 12-$17

What does it tell you when the eating is just steps off one of Hawai'i's major tourist thoroughfares, but still the clientele is 60 per cent local? Simple: it says the food's good, the prices right, and the service both professional and cordial. As owner Vong Chankhamany has been able to say since he bought the business more than a dozen years ago, "We have a really, really good local base." What might be Lahaina's best Thai cuisine is hidden in an end store at the Old Lahaina Center off Front Street, but it's not hard to spot because usually people are hanging around outside waiting for a table. Flavors and aromas hit you as soon as you walk into the small room, decorated in mirrors, Thai handicrafts, and linen-covered tables. The menu's large, but any one of the very good wait staff can narrow it down. Thai curry with peanut sauce features a Penang red curry paste, its vegetables, basil, and ground peanuts simmered in coconut milk. Pink snapper in lemon sauce with bell peppers, peas, and carrots in a tangy sauce of lemon and garlic comes to the table delicate and flavorful, and sautéed chili with a choice of meats is mixed with black mushrooms, bamboo shoots, onions, bell peppers, basil, and carrots. One especially yummy appetizer is two stuffed chicken wings, beautifully crisp and crunchy, stuffed with long rice noodles, onions, cabbage, and carrots. 'Ono! A suggestion: even if you think you're pretty macho, when the choice of spicing is mild, medium, or hot, do get at least one mild dish. You may appreciate it.

Bottom Line: Some of the best in Thai food, well served and decently priced.

KITADA'S KAU KAU CORNER

3617 Baldwin Ave. • 572-7241
Monday–Saturday 6 a.m.-1:30 p.m.
BYOB? No • Credit cards? No
per person: $3-$6

Baldwin Avenue, the main downtown street in this heavily gen-trified plantation community, in recent years has become a mélange of boutiques, galleries, and spiffed up eateries. But inside at least one of the original faded wooden storefronts nothing has changed. Not even an ounce of spiff has been added since Takeshi and Suteko Kitada opened their doors fifty-eight years ago and dished up the first bowl of noodles—unless you consider selling t-shirts to be upgrading. On Maui, when you say "Makawao" and "noodles" in the same sentence, the immediate response is still, "Ah, Kitada's." The founders have died, but family member Ethel "Nobu" Hotema still presides over the large steaming pots on the stove in the back and the continual flow of customers that comes through the swinging front doors. The guy sitting next to me on a bench one morning has been "eating here since [he] was eight," and he's nearly fifty. Seating is about two dozen on old benches and tables set on a cement floor, the counter is covered with a broad selection of candy bars, and the walls are plastered with family pho-tos. Food choices are simple, mostly broths: *saimin* made from their own *dashi*, plus a dry *mein* with broth on the side. Another hearty choice is the vegetable and meat omelet, more a scramble than an omelet, loaded down with cheese, your choice of meat (sausage, Spam, teriyaki, etc.), and mushrooms, onions, zucchini, and tomato. Although they're not on the printed menu, regulars know to order from a limited selection of plate lunches, especially an appetizing favorite such as tofu and beef.

Bottom Line: Good noodles and plenty of authentic atmosphere in a delightful old-time joint.

SAM SATO'S INC.

1750 Wili Pa Loop • 244-7124
Monday–Saturday 7 a.m.-2 p.m.
BYOB? No • Credit cards? No
per person: $3-$7

Noodle stories on Maui nearly always begin with Sam Sato. We assume Sam's making noodle soups these days in a more heavenly environment than Wailuku, but he opened his first noodle shop in 1933 and now, three moves later, succeeding generations are still behind the counter, often serving customers who remember noodling in the first shop. "From small I was there," says Cynthia at the next table. The bowls at Cynthia's table are by no coincidence the best selections in the house: succulent dry noodles with an order of soup on the side. Cooked with green onions, *char siu,* and bean sprouts, they're delicious. Look around and you'll see that the other regulars—and there are tons of them at this newest location in The Millwork light industrial and office complex—are enjoying the same thing, although *saimin* laced with *shoyu,* pepper, or Tabasco sauce is another popular choice. At breakfast another popular selection is banana pancakes, and all day long the display cases are emptying of flaky coconut, pineapple, pineapple and peach, and peach and blueberry turnovers, and lima or azuki *manju.* On the side: a wonderfully inexpensive BBQ teri beef stick. These days, Sam's shop is six stools at the counter and a mixture of wood-trimmed booths and tables, and on weekends you're likely to be waiting in line. The place is like home to a lot of Mauians, filled with laughter and chatter, kids and old men and women, all feeling like they're settling in at a friend's house with a tasty bowl of noodles and some soup.

Bottom Line: The premier noodle house on Maui lives up to its reputation.

GLOSSARY

adobo Filipino dish of chicken or pork simmered in a sauce of vinegar, garlic, and bay leaves.

'ahi Yellowfin or big-eye tuna, with red flesh, high fat content, and bold flavor, making it ideal for frequent use as sashimi or *poke.*

aku Skipjack tuna, with a deep red firm flesh and strong, acidic flavor, eaten raw, grilled, or dried.

akule Big-eyed scad, frequently grilled, fried, dried, or smoked.

anago Conger eel or sea eel, often served on top of rice or as sushi. Freshwater eel is called *unagi.*

banh hoi Very thin, hairlike rice noodles often served with Vietnamese grilled pork.

bao Chinese steamed buns, known in Hawai'i as *manapua.*

barbecue Hawaiian meat preparation, usually grilled, sometimes pan-fried.

bento Japanese box lunch separated into compartments for rice, meat, fish, pickled vegetables, and other items.

bi bim bap Korean dish of beef and assorted seasoned vegetables atop a bed of rice, topped with a fried egg and spicy sauce.

bulgogi Korean barbecued beef, thinly sliced and marinated in *shoyu,* garlic, ginger, sugar, green onions, sesame oil, and seeds.

butterfish Black cod, frequently salted and used in *laulau,* or prepared with miso sauce.

char siu Chinese barbecued pork, flavored with hoisin and colored red.

chicken luau Chicken, coconut milk, and luau, or taro leaves, cooked together like a stew.

chile water Spicy condiment of chile peppers, garlic, vinegar, and water often found on Hawaiian tables.

chop suey A term meaning "all mixed up," referring to a stir-fried Chinese dish of meat and vegetables.

chow fun Wide Chinese rice noodles, usually stir-fried with meats and vegetables.

chow mein Wheat noodles often stir-fried with vegetables and meat.

choy sum Chinese flowering cabbage, a bright-green leafy vegetable with yellow flowers.

cone sushi Vinegar-flavored rice with bits of carrots and green beans in pockets of fried bean curd; also called *inari* sushi.

congee Chinese rice gruel, also known as *jook*, eaten with an array of condiments as a breakfast or late-night snack.

daikon White radish common in Korean and Japanese dishes, often pickled.

dashi Basic Japanese stock flavored with seaweed and *katsuobushi,* used in a variety of ways.

delicatessen Takeout food store featuring a multitude of dishes from which to make a plate lunch; no relationship to sandwiches or New York.

dim sum Chinese for "dot the heart," referring to a variety of steamed, fried, or baked Chinese dumplings usually eaten with tea for breakfast or lunch.

dnardaaraan Filipino Ilocano dialect name for a dish of meat, intestines, and pork blood, known as *dinuguan* in Tagalog.

drive-in A place to get a hamburger, local specialties, or a plate lunch; little parking.

dynamite Mayonnaise-based topping on rice and/or fish layers, usually browned under a broiler and served warm in sushi bars.

'Ewa Direction, meaning toward town of 'Ewa from Honolulu, or northwest.

fish cake Japanese-style fish processed and pressed into a cake and steamed or fried.

furikake Japanese seasoning of bits of dried seaweed, sesame seeds, ground dried fish, salt, and other seasonings, usually sprinkled on top of rice.

gau gee Large, rectangular Chinese won tons filled with pork, seafood, or other ingredients, served in broth or deep-fried.

geso yaki Grilled squid tentacle.

gobo Burdock root, often prepared with carrots, dried shrimp, and *shoyu*, sometimes used in soups, stews, and sushi.

guisantes Filipino meat dish, usually pork, with peppers, tomatoes, and peas.

half moon Hawaiian term for a steamed half-circle dumpling of minced meat and/or vegetables in a translucent wheat-starch wrapper.

143

hamachi Yellowtail, or Japanese amberjack, often used for sushi.

hamachi kama Yellowtail collar, served fried or broiled.

haole Local word for white or Caucasian, sometimes used in a negative context.

haupia Coconut milk pudding thickened with arrowroot or cornstarch, served in squares at a luau; Hawaiian dessert.

Hawaiian sweet bread Portuguese sweet bread, an eggy, rich bread also referred to as *pao doce.*

hoisin sauce Sweet, thick Chinese sauce made of soybeans, sugar, vinegar, garlic, and spices, often used as a base for barbecue sauces for meats.

holokū Long, loose, seamed dress, often with a train, patterned after missionary Mother Hubbards.

huli huli **chicken** The trademarked name for chicken seasoned in *shoyu*-based marinade, turned often on an open grill, frequently sold roadside for school or charity fundraisers.

ika geso Squid tentacles.

imu Traditional Hawaiian underground pit oven, lined with hot stones and ti and banana leaves for cooking whole pigs and other foods.

izakaya Traditional-style small Japanese tavern or pub serving drinks and a variety of small dishes of vegetables, meat, seafood, and sometimes sushi.

jook Chinese rice gruel, also known as *congee,* eaten with an array of condiments as a breakfast or late-night snack.

joong Chinese triangular-shaped steamed packet of sticky rice wrapped in ti leaves that includes pork, shrimp, duck egg, mushrooms, and seasonings.

jun (juhn) Korean dish of thin slices of meat, fish, or vegetables fried in a light egg batter.

kai choy Chinese for mustard greens, often used in soups or pickled.

kakiage A kind of Japanese tempura in which small bits of fish, seafood, or vegetables are fried together as a clump.

kal bi Korean short ribs, sometimes butterfly cut, marinated in *shoyu*, garlic, green onions, and sesame oil and seeds, usually grilled.

kālua **pig** Traditional Hawaiian pork with a smoky, salty flavor, usually pig roasted whole in an *imu* and served shredded.

kamaboko Fish cake, sometimes bordered in pink, used in a variety of Japanese dishes.

katsu Japanese dish of breaded, deep-fried pork or chicken cutlet.

katsuobushi Dried bonito flakes used as flavoring in Japanese dishes and *dashi*.

kau kau Hawaiianized Chinese word for food.

kiawe Hard Hawaiian wood fuel used for grilling, similar to mesquite.

kilawen Filipino dish of meat or seafood pickled in acids like vinegar or *calamansi* (tart citrus) juice to cook the flesh.

kim chee Korean national dish, a pickle of napa cabbage, daikon, or other vegetables seasoned with garlic, salt, and chile peppers.

kitsune Japanese fried bean curd, served in broth.

kukui nut Candlenut, used in a relish called *'inamona*, made of cooked candlenut mashed with salt.

kūlolo A sweet baked or steamed Hawaiian pudding of grated taro and coconut cream.

laab Thai salad of ground or minced red meat or chicken with onions or shallots, fresh herbs, and ground roasted rice.

laulau Hawaiian dish of pork, fish, and/or chicken encased in taro leaf, wrapped in ti leaves, and steamed for several hours.

lechon Filipino-style roast pig, usually roasted on an open spit and traditionally seasoned with lemongrass and garlic.

liliko'i Hawaiian name for passion fruit, a tart, intensely flavored fruit with yellow-orange pulp and many black seeds.

limu A variety of edible seaweeds, frequently used in *poke* and salads.

loco moco Hawaiian-style hamburger patty served with rice and egg and smothered in brown gravy, usually eaten for breakfast or lunch.

lomi salmon Hawaiian dish made with diced salt salmon, onions, and tomatoes and *lomi lomi*-ed (mixed) with the hands.

long rice A soupy dish of mung bean or cellophane noodles, prepared with chicken, ginger, and green onions in broth; traditional at a luau.

look fun Steamed rice noodles formed in sheets, with bits of pork, shrimp, or green onions, eaten as dim sum or plain, cut into noodles for *chow fun*.

luau Hawaiian celebratory feast of food and festivity; also the leafy tops of taro.

lumpia Deep-fried Filipino spring roll of lacy egg-and-wheat-flour crepe, usually filled with vegetables and pork.

lunchwagon Traveling delicatessen serving plate lunches, found at parking lots, roadsides, beaches, and parks.

lup cheong Reddish, savory-sweet Chinese sausage seasoned with honey, sugar, salt, spices, and rice wine.

mahimahi An island fish, sometimes called dolphin fish or dorado, with a firm, light pink flesh, meaty and silky when cooked.

makai Direction, meaning toward the ocean.

maki sushi Rolled sushi, wrapped in nori, with egg, carrots, tuna flakes, and vegetables.

malassada Eggy, yeasty Portuguese fried doughnut without a hole, rolled in sugar, similar to a beignet.

manapua Chinese buns with fillings (chicken, pork, etc.), baked or steamed; common island snack.

man doo Korean dumplings filled with meat, tofu, and vegetables, served in broth or fried.

manju Japanese pastry of flaky crust filled with sweet beans, coconut, sweet potato, or other sweetened items.

mauka Direction, meaning toward the mountains.

mee krob Thai crisp-fried rice noodles in a piquant sweet-and-sour sauce flavored with garlic, pork, and seafood.

mein Chinese wheat noodle.

milo A tree planted in seaside locations; its rich brown wood takes a high polish and is prized for food containers and platters.

miso Fermented soybean paste used most often in Japanese and Korean soups and stews.

misozuke A sauce of miso, sake, and sugar often used with fish like 'ahi or butterfish.

mochi rice Sticky, sweet glutinous rice, frequently used in Japanese and other Asian sweets.

mochiko chicken Chicken coated in sweet, glutinous rice flour and fried.

musubi Triangle or ball of rice, usually wrapped with a piece of nori, often made with Spam or teriyaki chicken.

muumuu Long, loose woman's gown commonly worn in Hawai'i.

na'au pua'a Pig intestine stew.

nabemono Japanese one-pot dish, usually cooked at the table.

nam prik Thai chile sauce that includes shrimp paste, garlic, pea eggplant, and fish sauce.

nori Crisp, dark, thin roasted sheets of seaweed used for wrapping sushi or *musubi.*

'ohana Hawaiian for family, kin group, extended family.

okazuya Japanese delicatessen selling a variety of dishes from which to select and combine for a plate lunch.

ong choi Chinese for water spinach, a leafy green with arrowhead-shaped leaves and hollow stems; used in Chinese and Southeast Asian cooking.

ono Wahoo, or king mackerel, fish with white, flaky, firm flesh of moderately intense flavor.

'ono Hawaiian word meaning delicious.

'opihi Hawaiian limpet picked off coastal rocks, slightly salty, usually eaten raw.

oyako udon Thick Japanese wheat noodles in broth, topped with chicken, egg, and onion.

panko Japanese coarse bread crumbs that fry up crisp and crunchy.

pansit Filipino noodle dish based on egg, wheat, or rice noodles, with meats or seafood and vegetables.

pastele Puerto Rican steamed masa (dough) of grated green banana, usually surrounding a savory filling of seasoned pork, olives, and tomato sauce, like a tamale.

phad thai Thai stir-fried noodle dish of rice noodles, shrimp, bean sprouts, egg, tofu, peanuts, and chile peppers.

phô Classic Northern Vietnamese beef noodle soup, usually with meats, fresh herbs, chiles, and limes to drop into broth.

pinacbet Filipino dish of "wrinkled" vegetables and shrimp.

pinapaitan Filipino dish of beef and peppers with bile as an ingredient.

pipikaula Hawaiian-style beef jerky, frequently seasoned with *shoyu* and chile pepper.

plate lunch Popular Hawaiian meal that includes helpings from a selection of meats and seafood, plus scoops of rice, macaroni salad, and sometimes potato salad.

plum sauce Sweet, spicy, tangy Chinese sauce for dipping, often served with duck.

poi Traditional Hawaiian starch staple, made from steamed or boiled taro root, pulverized to a smooth paste and sometimes fermented before eating.

poke Hawaiian word meaning to cut into small pieces; often refers to raw fish or seafood cut into small pieces and marinated with such ingredients as *shoyu*, *limu*, *kukui* nut, onion, sesame oil, salt, and chile peppers.

ponzu **sauce** Japanese mixture of *shoyu* with acidic citrus fruits such as lemon.

pork hash Dim sum dumpling of finely chopped pork, water chestnuts, and seasonings, known also as *shu mai*.

Portuguese sausage Spicy, garlicky pork sausage, also called *linguiça*.

pot stickers Fried and steamed Chinese dumplings filled with pork and/or vegetables, also referred to as Japanese *gyoza*.

pūlehu Hawaiian cowboy-style meat, usually short ribs, steak, or chicken, marinated with Hawaiian salt and any combination of pepper, garlic, *shoyu,* or chiles, grilled or barbecued.

pupus Hors d'oeuvres or snacks (from the Hawaiian word *pūpū*, meaning snail).

saimin A uniquely Hawaiian noodle soup dish, originally Chinese noodles in a Japanese *dashi*, topped with Spam and/or *char siu* and green onions.

sake Japanese rice wine.

sarciado Filipino dish of meat or seafood with tomatoes, thickened with eggs.

sari sari Filipino stew of vegetables with bits of meat or seafood, seasoned with fish sauce.

sashimi Thinly sliced raw fish, usually dipped in *shoyu* and/or wasabi.

shabu shabu Japanese dish of meat and vegetables cooked in hot broth.

shiso Japanese herb also known as beefsteak leaf or perilla, a member of the mint family, often served with sashimi or in sushi.

shoyu Japanese for soy sauce.

shu mai Small steamed Chinese dumplings, also called pork hash.

soba Thin Japanese buckwheat noodle.

somen Fine Japanese wheat noodle, often served cold.

sukiyaki Hot Japanese stew-like dish of meat and vegetables served in soy-based broth.

sushi Japanese rice flavored with rice vinegar and topped or rolled around a variety of seafood and/or vegetables.

tako Japanese for octopus.

taro An underground tuber, starchy and potato-like, that can be dried and ground into flour, sliced thin and fried into chips, or mashed into a starchy paste known as poi.

tataki A Japanese method of preparing fish, especially *aku*, briefly grilled, leaving the center raw, then sliced thin like sashimi and served with a dipping sauce.

teishoku A Japanese set meal or fixed menu selection of dishes.

tempura Japanese preparation of seafood, meat, or vegetables coated in a light, lacy egg batter and deep-fried.

teriyaki (teri) Japanese sauce of soy, ginger, and sugar used for marinades and flavorings.

ti leaves Local plant leaves used for wrapping foods, especially luau items for cooking, and for adding flavor.

tofu Soybean curd used in various forms in Asian cooking.

toro Belly flesh of tuna, prized for its rich fat content.

tsukemono Japanese pickled vegetables, served alongside rice.

udon Thick, soft Japanese wheat noodles, usually served in broth.

ume Japanese salty, pickled plum, frequently eaten with rice and often found in the center of a *musubi*.

uni Sea urchin, prized for its ovaries, served as sushi.

vinha d'alhos Portuguese pickled pork, chicken, or fish, marinated and cooked in vinegar, garlic, and chiles.

wasabi Hot green Japanese horseradish served with sushi and sashimi.

won ton (wunton) Chinese dumpling stuffed with ground pork, served deep-fried or in soup.

yook kae jang Korean soup of shredded beef and long rice seasoned with chili peppers, garlic, and sesame oil.

ALPHABETICAL INDEX BY RESTAURANT NAME

★= Da Bes'

151